Tell Me Everything

OTHER BOOKS BY MARILYN MEBERG

I'd Rather Be Laughing

Choosing the Amusing

The Zippered Heart

The Decision of a Lifetime

Assurance for a Lifetime

Since You Asked

God at Your Wits' End

Free Inside and Out (with Luci Swindoll)

Love Me Never Leave Me

What to Do When the Roof Caves In

Tell Me Everything

How you can heal from the secrets
you thought you'd never share

MARILYN MEBERG

THOMAS NELSON
Since 1798

NASHVILLE   DALLAS   MEXICO CITY   RIO DE JANEIRO

Published in Nashville, Tennessee, by Thomas Nelson. Thomas Nelson is a registered trademark of Thomas Nelson, Inc.

Page design by Mandi Cofer.

Thomas Nelson, Inc., titles may be purchased in bulk for educational, business, fund-raising, or sales promotional use. For information, please e-mail SpecialMarkets@ThomasNelson.com

Unless otherwise noted, all scripture references are taken from *Holy Bible*, New Living Translation. © 1996, 2004, 2007. Used by permission of Tyndale House Publishers, Inc., Wheaton, Illinois 60189. All rights reserved.

Scripture quotations marked ESV are taken from THE ENGLISH STANDARD VERSION. © 2001 by Crossway Bibles, a division of Good News Publishers.

Scripture references marked KJV are taken from KING JAMES VERSION of the Bible.

Scripture references marked MSG are taken from *The Message* by Eugene H. Peterson. © 1993, 1994, 1995, 1996, 2000. Used by permission of NavPress Publishing Group. All rights reserved.

Scripture references marked NIV are taken from HOLY BIBLE: NEW INTERNATIONAL VERSION®. © 1973, 1978, 1984 by International Bible Society. Used by permission of Zondervan Publishing House. All rights reserved.

Scripture references marked NASB are taken from NEW AMERICAN STANDARD BIBLE®, © The Lockman Foundation 1960, 1962, 1963, 1968, 1971, 1972, 1973, 1975, 1977, 1995. Used by permission.

Scripture references marked NKJV are taken from THE NEW KING JAMES VERSION. © 1982 by Thomas Nelson, Inc. Used by permission. All rights reserved.

Some chapters of this book are reprinted, with editing, from the following Marilyn Meberg volumes published by W Publishing Group, a Division of Thomas Nelson, Inc., P.O. Box 141000, Nashville, Tennessee 37214: *The Zippered Heart*, © 2001; *Since You Asked*, © 2006. Used with permission. Other chapters are reprinted, with editing, from the following Marilyn Meberg volumes published by Thomas Nelson, Inc., P.O. Box 14100, Nashville, Tennessee 37214: *Assurance for a Lifetime*, © 2004; *God at Your Wits' End*, © 2005; *Love Me Never Leave Me*, © 2008; *What to do When the Roof Caves In*, © 2009. Used with permission.

Library-of-Congress Cataloging-in-Publication Data

Meberg, Marilyn.
  Tell me everything : how you can heal from the secrets you thought you'd never share / Marilyn Meberg.
    p. cm.
  ISBN 978-1-4002-0274-4
  1. Christian women—Religious life. I. Title.
  BV4527.M4365 2010
  248.8'6082—dc22

2009047268

Printed in the United States of America

10 11 12 13 14 WCF 7 6 5 4 3 2

I want to dedicate this book to my wild
and wooly friend Luci Swindoll.
She has harbored my secrets for nearly forty years
and as far as I know, not told anybody anything!

CONTENTS

ONE

Sweet Baby, Are You Hiding a Secret?

Last year a woman in the Midwest was troubled by recurring bouts of illness that she couldn't quite understand. The acute attacks of nausea, pain, and lethargy seemed to come out of nowhere without any obvious cause. She hadn't been around others who were ill; she hadn't eaten anything that would have caused physical upset. Yet again and again, the horde of mystery ailments struck, knocking her out of commission for a day or two, occasionally causing her to miss work or some family activity.

She probably should have gone to the doctor, but money was tight and the symptoms passed relatively quickly. Her physician was constantly booked, so it was hard to get an appointment. By the time she could get in to see him, she would be fine again, she reasoned. It also seemed silly to tie up the doctor's time with such short-lived problems—and doubtlessly cause herself to endure far more medical tests than she wanted to even contemplate.

And there was one more thing: she was afraid of what those tests might find.

This situation continued for several months. Then came the day, one morning last fall, when the sun rose but the woman couldn't. She'd spent a long night tossing and turning in her bed, unable to find relief from the achiness that filled her body and was so hot with fever she felt completely consumed by it. A widow, she lived alone. She phoned her office to say she wasn't coming in, and the perceptive co-worker who took her call was shocked at the woman's weak voice and what sounded like a strenuous effort to produce any words at all.

"I'm calling 911," she said. And she did.

The paramedics responded and, while taking the woman's vital signs, were alarmed to see that her temperature was 104 degrees. They carefully delivered her to the hospital, where the emergency personnel performed that battery of tests she had been avoiding. It didn't take long to discover the problem.

"You have a massive infection," the doctor told her. "It seems to have started in your kidneys or bladder but now has spread throughout your body and is affecting every system."

It was a slow-growing but vicious infection, the physician said, one that had probably been growing within her for more than a year.

4

"Haven't you been sick?" the doctor asked her.

"Yes," she said, "sometimes I've been sick. But then the symptoms would go away. I guess I knew something was wrong, but I just didn't want to think about it. I didn't want to go through all the tests I thought would be needed to diagnose such a strange problem."

The woman's reluctance to seek help almost caused her death. As it is, she's now coping with irreversible kidney damage that could have been prevented if only she had sought help sooner.

Secrets Cause Sickness

Like that dear woman, many people today are living with an unknown and undiagnosed infection that's silently growing inside them, causing them pain and suffering. They're afraid to think about it, talk about it, or let someone help them diagnose and treat it because they're afraid of the process—and afraid of what might be revealed. As a result, their happiness, their productivity, and sometimes even their lives are threatened.

The infection that was attacking the dear woman described here was caused by physical bacteria, but other types of infection can cause equally devastating pain and torment. Some of those infections are emotional rather than physical. One of the most destructive emotional infections can be a dark, venomous secret hidden within one's heart.

Maybe it's an addiction. As I write, the news is telling (and retelling) the horrifying story of a car crash in which eight people, including several children, were tragically killed. The crash was blamed on a "normal" suburban mother, also killed in the crash, whose blood tests revealed a shocking secret: the woman was not only drunk but also high on marijuana as she drove her minivan full of kids the wrong way on a New York freeway.

Perhaps it's a behavior. In her 2009 message to Women of Faith audiences around the country, my dear friend and co-worker Sheila Walsh shared how her discovery of her husband's secret, out-of-control spending had wrecked their finances and destroyed the trust on which their marriage had been established.

It might be an incident that occurred sometime in the past that seems too horrific now to even think about, let alone share. You might not even actively remember the incident, yet it's hidden there in your heart, oozing emotional and even physical infection capable of affecting every facet of your life.

Maybe it's not even *your* original secret; maybe your life is infected by a loved one's secret that you are desperate to keep secret too. Perhaps you're a pastor's wife, and someone in your family—perhaps even your husband—has made a mistake that would cause major upset if it were made known to the congregation. Maybe you're convinced that if the truth were known, your husband would lose his job and your family would lose its home and its only source of income.

This kind of infection sourced in dark secrets can be lethal to your happiness, a roadblock to your contentment. Its poison can burple up through the layers of your emotions, undetected, to cause you to respond in bizarre ways to ordinary events—and then it can disappear as mysteriously as it appeared. Or its fermenting poison can permeate your daily moments silently and invisibly—until eventually the venomous infestation becomes completely disabling, precipitating an emergency response and sometimes revealing irreparable damage.

In short, secrets can make you sad—and even sick.

Healing Secrets to Live Abundantly

A sad, sick life is not what God had in mind for you when He first thought up the idea of creating you. That was a long time ago, by the way, before you were capable of conscious thought. Before your parents ever met. In fact, it was before Adam and Eve ever met. It was before *everything!*

John 17:24 says, "You loved me even before the world

7

began!" And Ephesians 1:4–5 elaborates on that amazing fact: "Even before he made the world, God loved us and chose us. . . . God decided in advance to adopt us into his own family by bringing us to himself through Jesus Christ. This is what he wanted to do, and it gave him great pleasure."

God thought you up before He flung the stars across the heavens, and that thought made Him happy. Then, several eons later, He sent His only Son to earth as a sacrifice to make sure, when you get lost, that you always have a way to get back home to claim your place in God's family.

Jesus is that *way*. He told His followers He had come to earth so they could have "more and better life than they ever dreamed of" (John 10:10 MSG).

If God has been happily thinking about you since before the world began, and if Jesus endured hell on earth so that you could have a better life than you ever dreamed of, don't you think you ought to do *your* part to make that high-priced, heaven-inspired "better life" happen?

If that's not the life you're living—if your joy has been jarred out of socket by destructive secrets hiding within your soul—I hope this book will help you understand how sharing those secrets—those deeply hidden, too-awful-to-think-about secrets you thought you could *never* share—can help you achieve healing so you can live the better life God wants you to have. The chapters ahead have been adapted and compiled from my previous writings to provide, in one volume, a guidebook focusing on how to identify, address, and heal from the destructive potential of the dark secrets lurking in so many hearts. You'll read about some of the most common, and most devastating, secrets that get hidden away. Perhaps you'll recognize your own dark secret described in the coming stories about hurting souls who have desperately tried to deny or hide what's lurking in the dark corners of their hearts, infecting their own lives with hurt and harm in the process. If you do, I hope you'll also benefit from the suggestions I offer to help you share those secrets in a safe environment so that your healing can begin.

Now, before we continue, I must acknowledge that there *are* secrets that are better left untold. For instance, if a loved one has died, is there any benefit in telling his or her grieving children about mistakes made years earlier—poor choices including such things as infidelities or wild behaviors during younger years? Maybe so, but probably not.

And there are secrets that *must* be kept. I laughed hearing about the wise and protective parents, thinking of today's frightening "stranger-danger" culture, who taught their young children, "If anyone ever tells you something and then says, 'Don't tell Mommy,' or 'Don't tell Daddy,' you must come *straight* to Mommy or Daddy and tell us what that person said to you!"

The young children in this large family learned their lesson well, but it had some unintended consequences. When their older siblings planned a surprise fortieth birthday party for Mom, they shared the plans with their preschool brothers but gave them strict instructions to not tell their mother about the secret goings-on. Those orders set off warning bells and remembered teachings in the boys' little heads, and they lost no time at all in running to Mom to spill the secret.

So the surprise party wasn't actually a surprise, but it was still fun. Mom made a big show of *acting* surprised.

Theology and Psychology: a Perfect Fit

I have a master's degree in counseling psychology and worked for years in the mental health field. I also taught women's Bible studies for years. I believe Christianity and psychology are a perfect fit. Through my years of working with hundreds of clients, the fact was reinforced to me daily that psychology does not heal. Only God heals. But psychology gives us categories and helps us understand the origins of our psychic wounds. And when we understand the wounds' origins, we become great candidates for God's healing.

I don't mean in any way to imply that God cannot heal

you unless you have personal knowledge of your problem's origin. God's sovereign design ultimately trumps everything in our lives, including our core hurts and pains. And of course He already knows everything about us, including "the secrets of every heart" (Ps. 44:21). But countless times I've seen God use someone—a pastor, an empathetic friend, or a mental health professional—to help another person who's stuck in denial, determined to repress the secrets that are wielding a powerful negative impact. His Word tells us God can "bring our darkest secrets to light and . . . reveal our private motives" (1 Cor. 4:5). I believe that many times this is accomplished through the help of someone to whom the person entrusts his or her dark secrets.

The sharing of these secrets brings about healing because sometimes these hurting souls can't see the source of their own pain and problems, and they wonder why life doesn't work. Then that trusted, skillful listener comes along and helps them realize they can begin the process of clearing up an emotional infection by acknowledging its source—which is oftentimes a dark, destructive secret hidden away in their heart—and bringing it before the Healer.

One day last fall, seemingly out of the blue, Max Lucado Twittered out a Tweet that succinctly nailed another kind of emotional infection, *fear*. He reminded his fellow Tweeters, "It's our duty to expose our fears, each and every one." Max's words arrived during the week preceding Halloween while I was putting this book together, and it tickled me to see his characterization of fears. They are "like vampires," Max wrote. "They can't stand the sunlight."

Ditto, I might add, for secrets. Both are heinous villains that stand between us and the good, full, abundant life God wants us to have. But their power exists only when they remain hidden away in the dark corners of our hearts. They fade to nothing when dragged out, sometimes kicking and screaming, to cower before the Son. We all have secrets, and as long as they stay hidden, they have power over us.

God seems to address that subject in Deuteronomy 32:7, when He told Moses to instruct the Israelites to "dig into the past, understand your roots" (MSG). Why is digging necessary? We need to understand the root causes of our behavior. That helps us make changes in our lives and to then ask God to heal what the digging reveals.

Go Ahead. You Can Tell Me

Throughout my various careers, first as a college instructor and then as a mental health worker and now as a Women of Faith speaker, I have appreciated the wide variety of personality whose life paths have crossed mine. One of my favorite things to do is to settle into a comfortable place for tea and talk with someone interesting. I find it fascinating to hear someone's story and probe a little bit into the workings of his or her mind.

Sometimes during these chats, I suspect there's something else the other person isn't saying. Something important that's hiding behind the cheerful banter or hiding beneath the serious recounting of a personal setback.

Sometimes my "therapist radar" even detects that the other person is probably lying, and I wonder why. What's going on in this person's heart that makes telling the truth fearful? If we can get to the source of those secrets, we can diagnose the infection and bring it before the Creator. Then it is almost inevitable that healing will occur, and a life will be changed.

The only reason healing might not occur is that God, in His infinite and mysterious wisdom, may have another plan for another time when healing will occur. We don't always know why God's timing unfolds the way it does. The irony is that God has secrets! Deuteronomy 29:29 says, "The LORD our God has secrets known to no one."

Sometimes He chooses to reveal them to us; other times, we are left to wonder and simply trust Him. He has said He wants us to have a life that's better than we can ever dream possible. Do you believe that? If you do, and if you are burdened by problems that are rooted in the dark secrets buried in your heart, you have the opportunity to expose those secrets to the truth of His love so that you can get on with living the life He wants you to have.

Before God called her home to heaven, my friend Barbara Johnson often said, "Secrets are to sickness as openness is to wholeness." Keep that fact in mind as you read through the chapters ahead. As you read I hope you'll imagine yourself sitting in that comfortable spot with me, sharing a cup of tea (if you prefer, I suppose you could sip coffee, although I can't imagine it having the same pleasurable effect), and opening your heart to my imaginary ear and God's powerful and loving light of truth.

Go ahead, honey. Tell me everything.

. . . .

Keep Talking

. . . .

1. Are you aware of a dark secret that is impacting your life? How does it manifest itself in your day-to-day activities?

2. What do you think would happen if you shared your secret with a trusted friend, pastor, or mental health professional? What is the worst thing that could happen? What is the best?

3. How would your life change if the secret you are hiding

could be resolved—if an addiction could be controlled or a destructive behavior could be stopped?

4. Try to imagine yourself living without this secret lurking in your heart. How would your life be different?

. . . . .

TWO

. . . . .

Opening the Door
on Our Secrets

*E*very human soul houses innumerable secrets. In *A Tale of Two Cities*, Charles Dickens wrote, "A solemn consideration, when I enter a great city by night, is that every one of those darkly clustered houses encloses its own secret; that every room in every one of them encloses its own secret, that every beating heart in the hundreds of thousands of breasts there, is, in some of its imagining, a secret to the heart nearest it."

I love to contemplate the mystery and complexity of humankind. Like Dickens, I'm intrigued by the thought that every human soul has secrets. And I've learned, in both my personal and professional life, that each soul has its own style of safeguarding those secrets—as well as a different degree of ease about allowing those secrets to step out from behind the curtain and be shared.

People may appear open and genuinely caring, yet

there may exist in their demeanor that certain ill-defined something that signals me I can get only so close and then . . . they gently close the door.

I've found that true even with my own family members.

My husband, Ken, was a very private person. His gregarious and charming manner implied easy access to his soul, but such was not the case. He was loving, kind, generous, and an utter delight, but much of his inner being remained a mystery to me. When he died of cancer at age fifty-one, I felt bereft of a full knowing.

The same was true of my mother. She, too, was warm and loving but private and reserved. Much of her remained "a secret to the heart nearest it." In a later chapter, I'll share with you the shocking story of some of my mother's long-hidden secrets and how they impacted her life and mine.

In contrast, my father was verbally open, emotionally accessible, and loved to talk at the level of intimate exchange.

My own personal inclinations about the secrets beating in the hearts of others and those beating within my own heart are to pour a cup of tea, pull up a chair, and chat. In my experience, both as a professional therapist and as a friend and family member, I've learned that some secrets can be dark and destructive—while others are hilarious and even entertaining.

The Secrets Game

One of the most fun parties Ken and I ever gave centered on a spontaneous comment he made early in the evening. He suggested that everyone tell a secret that was embarrassing, but not so humiliating that he or she would object if Ken shared it with everyone he met the next day.

There were two persons whose secrets sent us all into unexpected gales of laughter. The first was told by a quiet and conservative man who generally observed his environment more than he participated in it. He blew us away with a recounting of how, in his senior year of college, he and his roommate rented a Cessna 182, stripped down to nothing but tube socks and tennis shoes, and then parachuted over their university campus. Because they drifted slightly off target, one touched down on the baseball diamond during the eighth inning of a well-attended game. The other landed on top of the administration building and was unable to escape without the aid of campus police.

The second favorite secret was told by a woman who had, with her husband, been a missionary in New Guinea for ten years. She said it is the custom among some tribes in New Guinea to greet a woman with a kiss on her bare left breast. With that information stated, she said no more. Ken asked, "What's the secret here?"

"Well, the secret is . . . I liked it!"

We all howled and clapped. Her husband's response was, "I wonder if that accounts for those easy conversions during our time there."

Probably the reason those two secrets were the party favorites was the secrets didn't match our perceptions of the secret holders. A conservative chemical engineer and a devout missionary allowed us to peek behind the curtain and glimpse their uncloaked humanity.

Handle with Care

Unlike the lightheartedness of those party secrets, many of us have learned that to reveal secrets can be disastrous and personally devastating. That was the experience of Sophie, Countess of Wessex, who is married to Prince Edward, youngest son of Queen Elizabeth. She was caught in a sting of enormous proportions. A reporter for Britain's *News of the World* posed as a sheik and potential client for the services of the public relations firm of which Sophie served as chairman. With hidden cameras rolling, Sophie was videotaped gossiping about her royal relatives—including additional possible marriages, the relationship between Camilla and Prince Charles (prior to their marriage), and how Sophie used her royal connections in ways that benefited her business.

That Sophie could stumble into such a royal mess came as a surprise because she, unlike Diana and Fergie, had until that time managed to avoid scandal. In fact, the media had considered her boring. She managed to change that image! Incidentally, she is no longer chairman of the board.

Not long ago, a young girl pulled a gun and opened fire in her school cafeteria. Another girl was shot and seriously wounded. Her offense? Telling the secrets of the shooter.

Our secrets are like porcelain: fragile and in need of careful handling. They can be fragments of our splintered selves, and we are wisely judicious before we risk placing them in someone's hands. That caution understood, what about the familiar refrains "We're as sick as our secrets" and "A secret has no power once it's told"? Is it healthy, wise, or necessary to share the deepest secrets of our hearts in order to free ourselves of the weight a secret can impose upon our souls? Is it not too risky to reveal those secrets that might damage our reputations if we dare to part the curtains?

Nathaniel Hawthorne's probing story *The Scarlet Letter* considers those questions through the characters of Hester Prynne and Arthur Dimmesdale. Hester was convicted of adultery by Boston's Puritan leaders; she gave birth to a child while serving her sentence in a local jail. Upon her release from prison, Hester was led to the town square, where she ascended a scaffold and, with her baby in her arms, suffered scorn and public admonishment. Condemned as an adulteress to wear a bright red letter A over her breast, Hester surprised the townspeople with her air of silent dignity.

She took up residence in a lonely cottage by the sea and came into town only when she had need of various supplies. Children jeered as she passed, other women avoided her, and clergymen pointed to her as a living example of the consequences of sin. Rumors circulated that she was a witch and that the scarlet letter she wore glowed a deep blood-red in the dark. Hester withstood the abuse without complaint.

Arthur Dimmesdale was a minister in the community who was deeply respected for his godly sermons and loved for his gentle, caring manner. Unknown to the community was the fact that he was the father of Hester's illegitimate child. He longed to confess his sin and resolve his intense sense of hypocrisy but was too afraid of the shame and ostracism open confession would bring. To make matters worse, the weaker and more guilt-ridden Dimmesdale became, the holier he appeared to his congregation. Every sermon he preached seemed to be more inspired than the last.

As the years passed, Hester, in spite of public disgrace and isolation, devoted her life to charitable service and won the hidden admiration of many of her peers. Dimmesdale, on the other hand, was increasingly weighed down by unbearable remorse even as his reputation for holiness increased.

One day, seven years after Hester's initial public censure, she came upon Dimmesdale walking through the woods at the edge of town. Speaking together for the first time since her trial and condemnation, Hester attempted to assure the minister that his good works and humility had gained him penance. But Dimmesdale cried out, "Happy are you, Hester, that wear the scarlet letter openly upon your bosom! Mine burns in secret!"

Because Hester's secret became known, she was not haunted by the fear of public exposure as was Dimmesdale. But in both cases there was great pain: Hester's public, Dimmesdale's private. In this instance perhaps the statements "We're as sick as our secrets" and "A secret has no power once it's told" hold true.

Actually, I think there is always a sense of relief that comes with a released secret. The issue is not whether the secret should be told, but to whom it should be told. I object to most public confession, which in my view tends to only deepen a person's shame and increase the potential of public ostracism. Unfortunately, very few people can be trusted to extend the grace that God so freely gives to His deeply flawed creations.

Some secrets can be kept private with no or little consequence. Whether or not to hold such secrets and protect them from public scrutiny is a matter of personal preference. As for me, I usually don't want to go public with all the sordid details of my life, but I do want to select a few close, kindred souls to know me and know my unattractive and even appalling secrets. I treasure their willingness to sit with me and invite me to tell them everything. There is nothing more liberating than being fully known and still loved.

To Tell or Not to Tell

Paul Valéry, the early-twentieth-century French poet, expressed a lifelong concern with the interior drama of our conflicting selves. He said, "A man who is of sound mind is one who keeps the inner madman under lock and key." It is safe to assume that Valéry would advise against the sharing of deep secrets. His stance may be the safer one to take.

The problem with the safer stance, however, is that it is also the lonelier stance. When we withhold ourselves from others, we have no intimacy—only a superficial veneer that poses as a relationship. Superficiality is fine for such activities as seeing a movie, watching a tennis match, or going out to dinner. But when I want to connect at the soul level, I seek out the person who really knows and loves me, and will share my life in all its rough and scratchy imperfections.

I have three completely trusted friends with whom I share my secrets. They know everything about me. Is that risky? I suppose it is, but time has proven these friends to be worthy of my trust. Time has also proven them to be available to me when I need more than a dinner companion. Because I choose to not live in emotional isolation, I believe I am far more enriched by the discreet sharing of my inner self than I am by remaining silent and unknowable.

Though I respect as well as honor anyone's right to manage secrets in a way that feels safe and maintains personal dignity, what troubles me about secrecy is this: many, if not all, of our secrets embarrass us. That's why they're secrets. We hope and pray no one ever finds out about them. Undoubtedly those kinds of secrets are emblazoned with the bright red letters that spell out "SHAMEFUL." So where do we keep those secrets? In our hearts behind a curtain that hides our hurts from others. There those secrets inspire such neurotic behavior as addiction, low self-esteem, mistrust, relationship dysfunction, depression, or eating disorders.

I'll give you an example of a secret that refused to remain behind the curtain. A few years ago I spoke at our Women of Faith conference about the masks we wear to cover the pain we feel. A woman came to my book table after I spoke and simply said, "My name is Becky. I'm a pastor's wife. I'm sick of my mask, and I'm sick of my life." I wanted to grab her, hug her, and hear her story, but she disappeared into the crowd before I even had a chance to respond.

I don't know if she felt she owed me an explanation, but I was thrilled to hear from her several days later. She described a portion of her pain to me. Becky had been fighting depression most of her life and bulimia for ten years. Jim, her pastor husband, knew about her depression but knew nothing of her bulimia; she had managed to keep that a secret. He was preoccupied with the needs of his fast-growing congregation, and Becky wanted to be a support to him rather than a hindrance. She taught a large Bible study for women each week and was in continual fear of "losing it" in front of everyone. When I saw her briefly at the conference, she was struggling to not lose it there in front of the fifty women she had brought from that study.

What happened in her life during the three years after our brief meeting is rather phenomenal. I have her permission to share some of it with you. Becky felt strongly that were anyone to know her two major secrets, bulimia and depression, she would be a "stumbling block" to people. As a pastor's wife, her faith could be called into question. She felt deeply responsible for maintaining a spiritually strong image for the sake of others. She also felt deeply ashamed. Why couldn't she get a grip? How could she keep living with a pressure that threatened to explode within her?

Sensing her husband's distancing from her, which she interpreted as indifference and potential abandonment, Becky broke down one evening (the one evening that week when her husband was home) and shared with him the secret of her bulimia. In great detail she described how she binged on ice cream, potato chips, doughnuts, cookies, and candy until she felt momentarily filled. Then she described the ritual of getting rid of it all by shoving her finger down her throat to bring it up. She told him about her self-loathing and her determination to never binge and purge again, only to find the cycle repeating itself over and over anyway.

As her husband, Jim, held his sobbing wife, he was stunned at what he'd heard but also a bit angry. He, too, thought she should get a grip and felt she would be a stumbling block to others. He felt her faith needed to appear strong for the sake of those whose faith was weak. Their partnership in ministry was built upon mutual belief in the need to model God's sufficiency for everything in life.

They prayed together for Becky and asked God to enable her to take Him at His word and not succumb to the weakness of her flesh. Becky felt enormous relief that Jim now knew about her bulimia. She determined that night to "get a grip." They both determined that, for the sake of others, Becky's bulimia must remain a secret.

As the weeks passed, Jim's preoccupation with church matters increased; Becky's determination to be strong diminished. Then, one Monday morning, her worst nightmare came true: she lost her grip in front of her Bible study. With wracking sobs, she confessed that she was a failure, that she suffered from severe depression, that she binged and purged at least three times a week, and that she could no longer pretend to be a model of spiritual strength. To her utter amazement, the words "I have failed God, I have failed my husband, I have failed all of you, and I am so ashamed" were followed by a mass movement of seventy-five women rushing forward to engulf Becky in loving support. They held her, encouraged her, and pledged to be instruments of healing for her.

Based upon the experience and recommendation of one of those women, Becky flew to Remuda Ranch in Wickenburg, Arizona, where, with the reluctant support of Jim, she entered one of the finest eating-disorder treatment centers in the country. Remuda specializes in a Christ-centered approach to helping women walk through the painful process of becoming whole. Becky learned how the loss of her mother to alcoholism and the subsequent abandonment by her father had laid the groundwork for her depression and eating disorder.

During the four months Becky was in treatment, she heard from at least two or three different members of her Bible study every day. These women continued to love her and support her in ways she'd never experienced in her life. She felt accepted, valued, and free to be "weak." She also recognized the tyranny her secrets had held over her heart.

One of the biggest changes in Becky's thinking was to realize that she didn't deserve to wear the shame banner. Her depression had an environmental root; it was not a sin and it was not her fault. Her challenge was to face her issues and be healed from them. Her bulimia was not a sin either. It was one of the many expressions of all the childhood pain she had never resolved. At Remuda that process of understanding and healing began.

Becky is once again teaching her women's Bible study, but she now has a new vulnerability. The women who attend have a new vulnerability as well. The group now has an atmosphere of love and receptivity that invites the sharing of souls and the sharing of secrets. The faith-based support system modeled by Becky's group is rapidly spreading to other segments of the church.

Jim has come to realize that his inordinate concern with looking good for the sake of others has had more to do with his own needs than with preserving God's image. He was deeply invested in having others think highly of him. When Becky left for treatment, he was embarrassed by her. He is slowly coming to realize that his own veneer of competency covers a vast chasm of insecurity. Becky jokingly told him that if he could just whip up an eating disorder, he could also go to Remuda Ranch and work through all the "stuff" in his chasm.

Earlier in this chapter I asked the question, "Is it not too risky to reveal those secrets that might damage our reputations if we dare to part the curtains?" Becky's story illustrates how she was able to get help only when her cover was blown through an inability to keep her own secret. Were it not for the parting of the curtains, Becky and Jim would both have continued their valiant efforts at maintaining their divided selves. Instead, they have grown personally and been healed in ways that encouraged the healing of others in their faith community.

Not only does Becky's story illustrate the healing potential of a secret shared, but it also illustrates that not all secrets deserve to wear the shame banner. Shame inspired Becky's behavior, but the shame itself was undeserved. You will find that shame and its resolution are major themes throughout this book. Shame is a toxic tenant of our hearts that we'll need every creative plan we can come up with to evict.

In the coming chapters we'll coax a few more common secrets out from hiding and into the light of God's grace as well as our understanding so we can see how they are influencing our behavior. We'll also take a look at what else might be standing in the way of our inclination to pull back the curtain.

Keep Talking

1. What is your style in safeguarding your secrets?

2. Do you agree or disagree with this statement: "A secret has no power once it's told"?

3. What is your opinion about public confession? Do you think this should be a practice in the church?

4. Have you ever been hurt by entrusting a secret to someone who later betrayed you by telling the secret? How has that experience shaped your level of openness with others?

5. Did you grow up with family secrets that were "not to leave the walls of this house"?

THREE

My Secrets
Fill Me with Shame

One summer a friend drove down to my rented California beach house for a day. Our plan was to walk to the village for lunch, come back to my house, change clothes, grab the beach umbrella, and then luxuriate for the rest of the afternoon on the sand.

As we headed out the door for town, I dropped the house key in the back flap of my beach chair, which leans against the wall on the front porch. My friend paused and said, "Don't tell me you're leaving your house key there!"

"Yes, I am! I always pop it in that chair flap. That way I don't have to rummage around in my purse looking for it when I come home."

"Well," she said, "it doesn't seem wise or safe to me, but of course that's none of my business."

Finding her words mildly irritating but also thinking she might be right, I put the key in my shirt pocket instead of the chair flap. I also remembered why I only saw her a few times a year.

Finishing lunch and a very one-sided conversation where I learned everything she had done, said, or thought in the last seven months, we returned home, changed clothes, and started for the beach. On the short walk there she said, "Now, you have your key, don't you?" Attempting to keep my claws retracted, I said, "Of course I have my key—it's in the flap of my beach chair!"

After another two hours of one-sided conversation, she announced how much she loved our chats but that she simply had to head for home. As we climbed the stairs to my front door, I attempted to find the house key in the side flap of my beach chair. In frustration I threw down the umbrella, the pole, and all the other stuff in my hands and on my back to better free myself for the key search. (Wouldn't you think she could have carried something?)

"Don't tell me you've lost the key," my friend said.

Trying hard to not hiss, I said, "Of course I haven't lost the key; I transferred it from my pocket after lunch. I distinctly remember putting it here—just give me a minute."

"You obviously did not transfer that key, or it would be there!"

"I most certainly did transfer the key. Maybe it fell out on the sand."

Rolling her eyes in exasperation, my friend trudged

back with me to our "spot" to comb the sand with our fingers. No key. We walked back home.

A sweet guy painting a house across the street lugged his long ladder over to my second-story unit and insisted that he, not I, scamper up the ladder and walk through the open French doors (another safety infraction according to my friend) that led to the front entrance. As we walked in, I sheepishly thanked him and with relief saw my friend to her car. As she was driving away, her parting shot was, "Better call a locksmith, Marilyn, and then, for goodness' sake, take better care of your key!"

Pleased that I had not yielded to the instinct to claw her face, I ran up the stairs and down the hall. Grabbing the blouse I'd worn to lunch, I checked the pocket. There was my key! Contrary to my vehement insistence, I really had not transferred the key to my beach chair's flap. My friend was right. I hated that! She was overbearing, self-absorbed, and demeaning; she did not deserve to be right!

All evening I hoped she wouldn't phone to see if I'd called a locksmith. I determined I would not admit to her that the key was in my pocket just as she had said it was. I even fabricated a great story about having returned to our sand spot where I met a wonderfully handsome, middle-aged man who compassionately helped me search through the sand and who found the key. We celebrated by having an intimate dinner later that evening. Carrying my fabrication even further, I imagined how he'd told me over dinner about the tragic death of his wife ten years ago and that I was the first woman he'd met since then who made him feel perhaps there was another love for him in the future. It was such a fun story, but of course I couldn't actually tell it to what's-her-face; after all, it was a complete and thoroughly compelling lie!

She called the next morning; I confessed. Her only comment was, "You really shouldn't live alone, Marilyn."

A Core Indictment

Admittedly, my former friend's attitude was not attractive, but what was my problem? Why should I so resist admitting the truth to her? It is of course always easier to be candid when the atmosphere is supportive and warm, but so what? The bottom line was I didn't want to be caught being wrong! Why? Because being wrong chips at my self-esteem; I look better to myself (and, I assume, to others) when I'm right. I don't look good when I'm wrong.

Where did those thoughts come from? From the internal nagging moral tracers that extend all the way back to the Garden of Eden. Disobedience of God's law started there with Adam and Eve, and we've been ashamed of ourselves ever since. The moral tracers cause us to be aware that we're not living up to what we were originally created for, which is perfection. We lost the experience of perfection, but we'll never lose the expectation of it. We think somehow we'll get it back if we just work a little harder.

In the meantime, we hope no one will notice the full scope of our imperfection. We come up with elaborate cover-ups to divert attention from our true state—diversions such as the delicious lie about the man who found my key and found me so incredibly charming that he thought true love might enter his life again. Now that's a little pathetic, if you ask me. But I salve my embarrassment at even thinking up that whopper in the first place by telling myself that at least I didn't actually tell the lie. Maybe there's hope for me. Hope for what? Perfection? No way.

Shame's Link to Secrets

The reality is I'm not perfect. Surprise! I misplace my house key, I let people down, I try to look better than I am, I don't always do what I say I'll do, I sometimes betray confidences, and on occasion I've been known to fudge on the truth. Am I proud of this short list? (Actually, I've got a longer one.) Of course not. I am, quite frankly, ashamed of myself. And that brings us to the whole point of this chapter. (Finally!)

The reason it is so hard for us to admit to the secrets hidden in our hearts is that we're ashamed of them. We think that if we keep denying our ugly stuff, then maybe we'll look better than we fear we actually are. We keep it a secret. And those secrets can fester and swell until they consume our happiness and our hope.

No matter how carefully we guard the secrets, no matter how creatively we scramble in our efforts to look good, we still suffer from that deep-seated sense of shame and will do almost anything to avoid it. But here's an important truth: shame is not what we do; it's who we perceive ourselves to be. Shame is a core indictment of our very essence.

The subject of shame has occupied the minds and writings of mental health professionals for the past few decades. As a result, many books and articles help us understand why our shame feels so shameful. Perhaps most helpful to our understanding is that at the very core of shame lives the panicked fear of abandonment and rejection. If you really knew me and the nature of the stuff that lives in that dark corner of my heart, you'd not only be shocked, but worse yet, you'd be appalled. If you're appalled, then I have every reason to assume you will reject me. If you reject me, I will experience abandonment, which is the most devastating emotional state in which to live.

One of the greatest driving forces of our nature is to

feel connected to other human beings. To truly experience connection is to experience oneness; without it, we can withdraw into a world of lonely isolation. To avoid isolation, rejection, and abandonment, we deny our left-side realities; they are simply too threatening to acknowledge.

I do have to point out, however, that in spite of shame's potential toxicity, not all shame is unhealthy. The capacity to feel shame is normal, adaptive, and a requirement for developing healthy guilt, a sensitive conscience, compassion, and empathy. Healthy shame develops in an environment that is basically loving and nurturing. Were it not for healthy shame, we would not be driven to our knees in recognition of our need of a Savior. We wouldn't lift our voices then in praise and gratitude for the forgiveness of sin and the grace that says we're cleansed.

But when our secrets become too powerful, shame becomes an identity, a state in which we feel different, despairing, and helpless. It then creates an interior environment in which the balance is lost between the healthy shame and unhealthy shame. This kind of unhealthy shame indicates that we've lost our true identity and value as God's creation whom He called into being out of love and with pleasure.

Can we blame our shame inclinations totally on the loss of perfection in Eden? No. Adam and Eve's sin was the root of our imperfection, but there are many layers that are laid on top of that foundation of original shame. Although there are many contributors to those layers of shame, they are usually laid first in childhood.

The Building Blocks of Shame

I believe most parents who have contributed shame to the junk pile of their kids' hearts have done so unwittingly. Without realizing the intense ramifications their words or actions may have upon the developing sense of self, parents can unintentionally do long-lasting damage.

When parents communicate to the young people in their home that they are loved and appreciated, those children assume then that they are valuable, worthy members of the family. That assumption translates into feelings of self-esteem so they do not find it hard to fathom they are lovable. For example, regularly using phrases such as, "I love you," "You are wonderful," "I am proud of you," and "You give me joy"—with accompanying hugs and kisses—builds a secure environment in which shame is rarely, if ever, experienced. When the child misbehaves and needs to be corrected, discipline can still be handled in an atmosphere of positive and unconditional love. Hopefully, the parents communicate that, though certain behaviors are unacceptable, the child is loved unconditionally.

Sadly, however, many children rarely, if ever, hear the words, "I love you" or "I'm proud of you." The parents may feel love for their child and may even be proud of her, but if the words are never spoken, the child does not experience affirmation. That lack produces insecurity. This kind of environment causes the child to think maybe she isn't lovable and maybe she is nothing to be proud of. Those thoughts open the door to shame—the private, core evaluation of the self.

I have a dear friend who was rarely hugged as a child and, to her memory, never praised. Her parents were well-meaning, basically nonverbal people who worked hard but had no idea how to communicate acceptance or love. The result is that my friend, now as an adult, never feels satisfaction with the quality of whatever she does. She continually berates her writing, her speaking, her appearance, and her value to her profession. There is always a little voice in her head that says, *You could do better, others write far better than you, and if you're going to be a public speaker, you'd better learn to express yourself more effectively*. The clincher message she hears in her head is, *You ought to be ashamed of that sloppy performance!*

That feeling of not being good enough carried over into her marriage. She is sure her husband must be disappointed with the kind of wife she turned out to be. According to her, he's too nice to say so, but in her heart she believes he wishes he'd never married her. That belief about herself was further underscored by the fact that she has not been able to have children. There doesn't seem to be a medical reason for the childlessness, but my friend is sure it's her fault.

Children initially have no measuring stick to use in determining their value except the reactions they get from their parents. Unlike the parents in the previous example, some parents are exceedingly verbal with their children, but their verbalizing is negative and critical. "If you can't say something nice, don't say anything at all." "I can't believe you haven't at least brought that reading grade up from a C. Your sister never got a C in her life. I guess it's obvious who has the brains in this family!" "You've got the worst-looking hair I ever saw—maybe we ought to just shave it all off!"

Some of the ways we produce a lack of personal worth and value (shame) in our kids are more subtle than the previous examples but nevertheless are damaging. Children can be made to feel like a burden, an intrusion, an irritation, or an inconvenience—even if the words are never spoken. Such messages can be communicated through repeated expressions of impatience and exasperation or by phrases like "I just don't have time" or "Please don't bother me right now; I have so much I need to do." To my utter chagrin and deep regret I used the phrase "I just don't have time right now" far too many times as our two children were growing up. As I look back, I have no memory of what great deeds I accomplished with my insisted-upon time, but I have a vivid memory of their disappointed little faces.

When parents have no time and are impatient and exasperated, they unintentionally plant shame seeds. If they seldom praise, frequently criticize, and rarely hug their child, the child's shame flourishes rapidly. And when the child is made to feel like a burden instead of a pleasure, the shame, like a creeping vine, trails her through life.

The bottom-line assumption made by any child who experiences these environmental lacks is that the problem lies with her, not the parents. The child, based on the evidence, simply decides she's a disappointment, a mistake, maybe even a total loser! If she's an inherently spunky little kid, she'll fight the messages and try to disprove them by concentrating on her performance, trying desperately to be the best in whatever. Let me give you an example.

In my first year of teaching, I had a classroom of especially macho third-grade boys with equally macho third-grade girls. I frequently wondered if the water supply in that neighborhood had been spiked with heavy doses of testosterone. I didn't know how else to account for their hurly-burly ways. What gave me a giggle was the fact that there was no bullying of the girls either on or off the playground. The boys knew that if there was just one unwanted behavior from any of them, the girls would simply deck him with one flashing fist to the jaw, step over his sprawled body, and continue playing jump rope. The result of all this was a very peaceful playground as well as classroom. (Ken suggested that rather than drink the water at the school during breaks and the lunch hour, I might want to take my own bottled water. I think he feared what I might become.)

Several weeks into the year, a new boy arrived from Mexico and was placed in my class. He spoke a little English and I spoke a little Spanish; the result was a fun series of gestures and drama. He told me his name was William. I foolishly called him Billy several times, I guess in an effort to establish greater familiarity. Whatever the reason, William began signing all his papers Billy William. He became Billy William then to everyone.

What concerned me about Billy William from the first day was the obvious lack of testosterone he exhibited. I worried his pudgy little body might become a target for my third-grade cave men and women the minute they all hit the playground. I was stunned to find how ill-founded my fears were. I watched during dodge ball in the morning, kickball at noon, and baseball in the afternoon, while Billy William tore around the playground as if he'd been goosed by an electric cattle prod. He ran faster, dodged more adroitly, and hit the ball farther than any of my little Neanderthals.

Curious to know what drove this little dynamo, I told his mother during our first parent-teacher conference that he was the best athlete in my class. She laughed and said, "No, no, not William; he a runt." I asked if there were other children in the home. "Oh yes: Pedro. Pedro big; Pedro smart; Pedro run and run and run."

The next day I asked Billy William about Pedro. Billy William's eyes lowered to his paper and then he whispered, "Pedro best."

I bent down and whispered, "I think Billy William's the best. He's fast as a race car!"

Billy smiled slowly. "Yeah . . . race car!"

From then on I no longer called him Billy William; I called him Race Car. He was soon signing his papers Race Car. And before long, my little Neanderthals were calling him Race Car as well. (Poor kid—I may have built his esteem, but he lost all name identification.)

As I attempted to envision the dynamics of his home life, it seemed safe to assume William was called "Runt" and probably received little recognition. It appeared that Pedro was the family hero; William was merely a presence. But rather than hang back and accept "runt" status, William rose up, determined to be better and faster than a runt.

Lots of kids manage to compensate and seemingly cancel out negative messages by excelling in various endeavors. Those are the kids with pluck and grit who refuse to be discounted. Even so, they are never sure they're good enough and often spend their lifetime trying to drown out the secret messages that were recorded in their brains early in life.

Incidentally, I was thrilled to learn years later that Billy William Race Car received a tennis scholarship from the University of Southern California. I didn't hear anything about Pedro.

Managing the Shame Pile

You may be tempted about now to say, "There, you see, Marilyn? Little Race Car made it in life. All you shrink types who constantly harp about the harm we do to our children give me fits. So Billy William didn't ever feel like 'the best.' It sure didn't seem to ruin him. He rose above it all. And rising above the negative is a necessity for living life! No one has a perfect background with perfect, smiling parents who know exactly how and when to discipline and just exactly how to make their child know the discipline was about his behavior and not his person."

And you're absolutely right! No one on the face of the earth can parent perfectly. Every single one of us can remember at least a bazillion times (I sure can) when we have blown it as parents. And yes, we all have to learn how to rise above the negative input we received as kids and continue to receive even as adults. But here's the point: The fact that we rise above the negativity and are outward successes is not the issue. The issue is that all the hurtful, shame-producing secrets that get hidden away in our hearts or our heads are not eliminated simply because we've managed to excel. The shame pile still exists, giving rise to secret self-talk that continually causes us to question our core value. As long as that shame-inspired self-talk goes on, we will work harder and harder to prove the secret internal messages wrong.

One of the many possible patterns that the shame mind-set can produce is workaholism: "Enough is never enough" is the thinking behind that pattern. No matter how hard the workaholic person performs or how successfully the goals are reached, he or she still has the sense that it could have been better.

The "enough-is-never-enough" shame voice also affects relationships. This person has trouble receiving love because she believes that somehow love, like everything else in life, has to be earned; she has to qualify. Simply hearing the words "I love you" sets off myriad internal responses, such as: "You wouldn't say that if you really knew me." "Once you know me you won't love me because I'm not as good or successful as I may appear." "It'd be safer for me to keep you at a distance so that you don't find out the truth about me." "I guess I'll marry you, but you'll never get very close to me because I've got to work very hard so you'll continue to think you love me because love is based upon what I do and not who I am. Besides, I have to work very hard just to feel good about myself, so no matter how you look at it, my first priority, my basic commitment, will be to my work. Doing well in life is what assures me I'm valuable."

Let me give you one more example of how shame can take up secret lodging in our hearts at a very early age due to, in this case, unwise mothering. (Before you drop the book and dash off to pour yourself a little cup of strychnine, this is the last negative example. I promise we'll conclude this chapter on a more upbeat note!)

My father was born into what he described as "a litter" of ten children. From his earliest memory he felt like an unwanted burden: yet another mouth to feed, another body to clothe and house. Repeatedly his mother told not only him, but all the children, that she wished they had never been born. It was her custom to reach out and smack whoever was closest at hand, hitting whatever part of the body was nearest, and say, "That slap was for whatever you shouldn't have done that I missed." It never occurred to her to make up for the hugs they all missed.

Many secret shame messages were etched into my father's psyche as he grew up, but one of the more pronounced was his shame for having needs. Since his and the other children's basic needs for food, shelter, and clothing seemed most to upset his mother, Dad, without being able to label it as such, felt he shouldn't have those needs and was ashamed that he did.

He determined very early in his life that as soon as he possibly could, he would leave home and tend to his own needs so he would no longer be a burden. At the age of thirteen, he did indeed leave home, vowing to never return. Out of respect for the poverty of his family, he sent a portion of his hard-earned wages as a sawmill worker to his mother each month. Slowly he earned enough money to leave eastern Canada and go to the United States, where he ultimately put himself through school and became a pastor.

Later, as Dad looked back on his childhood, he understood his mother a little better. She had ten children by the time she was thirty-five. Her husband, who was a tender man but in poor health, was able to provide very little for the family. Responsibility for everyone's well-being rested upon this young mother's tired and overworked shoulders. They barely survived. Dad felt regret for her hard life but felt no love for his mom. He had no desire to ever see her again, especially after his kindly father had died.

I well remember meeting this grandmother for the first time when I was fourteen. She was determined to make the long trip from eastern Canada to Washington state because

Jasper (my father) was the only son who'd never come home. She had not seen him in thirty-one years.

My grandmother was a little fireball of a woman with eyes so blue they were nearly black; they literally sparkled with intensity and humor. I shared my bedroom with her, and we laughed and giggled late into the night during her five-day visit. One day she tried to teach me how to make an apron. When I sewed the pocket on upside down (which kept it perpetually empty), my grandmother laughed so hard she simply collapsed on the floor. I loved her.

The day she left she attempted to give some money to my father. He politely but coldly refused it, saying, "I have no needs, Mother."

Her response was, "Please take it; it's for all the times I missed."

He again refused it and, with a formal handshake, put her on the train.

As we drove away from the train station, my mother turned to Dad and said quietly, "Why, Jasper, it would have meant so much to her for you to take the money."

His curt response was simply, "It's too late."

I was utterly mystified by the behavior of my normally warm, fun-loving father. In fact, I hadn't been able to figure out why he had treated his mother with such cold courtesy all week. As far as I was concerned, she was wonderfully fun, loving, and great to be with. I had also noted that my mother was extremely kind and solicitous toward her. What in the world was wrong with my father?

Now, years later, I know what was wrong with my father, and the knowledge breaks my heart. All Dad knew as a little fellow was that he was unwanted and a burden. In addition, he was mistreated. It never occurred to him that he was in reality a gifted, delightful child who was lovable and capable of being a joy to any mother. Neither did it occur to him that this inherently warm and fun-loving mother was so desperately overwhelmed as well as unschooled in parenting skills that she was unable to cope. No child understands that kind of complexity. The only message that was seared into Dad's psyche with the intensity of a branding iron was that he was a person unworthy of even the food, shelter, and clothing he so desperately needed to survive. Unable to fend for himself regarding those basic needs, Dad assumed there was something wrong with needing—something wrong with him, not with his mother and not with their circumstances. In his mind, he was nothing more than an inconvenience and a burden. Shame took up residence in Dad's heart and never left.

The result was that Dad never reconciled with his mother and never forgave her for her inability to parent under crushingly adverse circumstances. In his mind he understood, but in his heart he remained unmoved. He hung on to his fierce independence and determination to need nothing from anyone until the day he died.

I so wish Dad had understood the insidiousness of the shame that prevented him from experiencing healing release, the freedom to forgive, and the God-given right to appreciate his true value. Even though he was an effective minister and sincere communicator of the gospel of grace, there was that one dark, secret corner of his heart that grace did not penetrate or heal.

Why? He didn't understand shame's crippling effects upon his life. He understood salvation and how it was attained through a relationship with Jesus Christ. He understood prayer and his need for spiritual communion. But he never understood or addressed the fact that he was housing a colossal secret, a vicious lie that hissed out demeaning messages about his worth. He attempted to drown out the messages by working harder, hoping to minister more and more effectively in the lives of others.

Tragically, I'm afraid that is true for so many of us. The shame that insists we have no value runs totally contrary to the Bible's message that says we are of such value to be worth the death of God's only Son on the cross. Over and over again in Scripture God declares His unfailing love and His unconditional caring for His creation, and yet that message more often than not falls on shame-deafened ears. In spite of the preaching of grace, shame is still an imperious presence in many of our hearts and our churches today.

The good news is there is a cure for imperfection that leads to shame, which causes us to live in denial and fear. The cure begins when we open our hearts to the light of God's love—and share what's hidden in that dark, secret corner.

Keep Talking

1. Discuss a time when you couldn't seem to admit to being wrong.

2. What are some of the elaborate cover-ups you use to divert recognition that you are less than perfect?

3. Can you pinpoint the first time you experienced shame?

4. Was your childhood home one in which you felt valued and affirmed? If so, what specifically did your parents do to make you feel valued?

5. Examine some of your behavioral patterns and determine if any of them springs from a shame base. Is it possible to change the behavior? How?

FOUR

Secrets and Mysteries
of the Mind

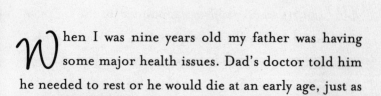

When I was nine years old my father was having some major health issues. Dad's doctor told him he needed to rest or he would die at an early age, just as his own father had died of a heart attack.

Following the doctor's orders, Dad resigned as pastor of what is now the United Methodist church in Amboy, Washington, and bought forty acres of utterly remote, heavily wooded, and spectacularly beautiful land about ten miles from town. I stayed in the same school but was no longer within walking distance of anyone or anything except the dense undergrowth of endless forests. A gorgeous creek ran through the property, meandering its way to somewhere I could not imagine but thought I'd like to go.

It was picture-perfect property. The population of those forty acres was three: Mom, Dad, and me. (It was four if I included my dog, King.) The low population count was exactly what Dad needed. His normally gregarious and social inclinations gave way to peace, quiet, and few people. In contrast, I have never in my life not needed people, so my gregarious and social inclinations died in the breeze rustling through the evergreen trees.

Mom was teaching at the school I attended, so we drove back and forth together each day. I loved that. She was a wonderful listener and was quietly present in the midst of my emotional flailing about. Two years later Dad sold "Lonely Acres" and was appointed to the pulpit of the United Methodist church in Manor, Washington. I loved it when we moved. I was instantly healed of all my accumulated neuroses as I rode my bike with Bev Smith, played basketball with Ed Charter, and listened to the love life of Ina Chapin. Who could ask for more?

Because Ken had heard the good, the bad, and the ugly about Lonely Acres, he wanted to see the place. It was a major side trip on our way to Seattle one summer day in June, early in our marriage, but we swung off the I-5 and headed for Amboy and Lonely Acres.

I had not seen the property in fourteen years, so as we traveled up Bosewell Road I felt warmly nostalgic. After all, there were good memories associated with Lonely Acres too. As we topped the hill at the end of Williams Road, we were enveloped by a dense undergrowth of trees nearly shrouding from view the little valley below. We got out of the car and looked down that long, winding road that dropped down into the valley where my former house was located near the meandering creek.

Suddenly I felt faint—nauseous and terrified. Nothing looked quite the same, but for some reason it *felt* the same.

Ken rushed over and helped me sit down. "What is it? What's wrong? You're shaking and pale. Marilyn, are you sick?"

I didn't have a clue what was wrong, but I had a sudden memory of standing in that very spot as a ten-year-old kid scanning the long driveway down to Williams Road waiting for my parents to come home. It was five o'clock. They were supposed to be home by four. Had they been killed? Was I now an orphan? Who would take care of me? We had no neighbors . . . no phone . . . I was the only child in the universe.

Reliving that forgotten memory, I was once again terrified. I threw up in the grass—in the very spot where I had thrown up fourteen years earlier. Fourteen years earlier, my dog, King, had comforted me. Now, as I relived my terror, it was Ken who did the comforting.

In reliving that memory, I remembered then the rest of the experience. About five fifteen my parents came tearing down Williams Road and topped the hill to find me sitting nonchalantly on the grass, waiting for them as if nothing were wrong. As I crawled into the car for the short trip down to the house, both parents apologized for being late, explaining that Mom had an unexpected faculty meeting that delayed her (and of course that was before cell phones).

I told them, "No problem. King and I just decided to walk up to wait for you." I never told them I'd been so terrified I'd thrown up and had tried to figure out how I'd live in an orphanage where, like Oliver Twist, I would need to beg for more gruel. I kept that fact a secret, tucking it securely away in that dark corner of my heart to be forgotten forever.

Or so I thought.

I didn't know it then, but the situation I had endured had sparked within me the terror of abandonment. I didn't deliberately hold it in my heart as a secret; I simply banished an unpleasant memory to the recesses of my mind. There it lived, dormant but real, as a dark, secret worry. Fourteen years later, the secret came out of hibernation, and I felt it again. The memory had not been summoned; it just came crashing through to my conscious mind.

The Unbidden Release of Buried Memories

What is often confusing about those images that suddenly reemerge is that they can seem unrelated to what is happening at the moment. But they are triggered by something in the environment that causes the unconscious to release the buried memory that has been held secret. There is always a purpose in that release, and that purpose is related to our ultimate healing from the hurt associated with that remembered experience. More about that later.

My daughter, Beth, had a similar experience when she, too, unintentionally relived an abandonment memory; hers was rooted in the very first hour of her time on earth, so it's no surprise that it remained a secret from her consciousness. What was surprising was the way it re-announced itself years later.

Beth was a young adult when she began her search for her birth parents. When she found them, she learned that they had been high school sweethearts when her birth mother, Sherry, became pregnant. They were too young to marry, and abortion was out of the question. But being an unwed mother was scandalous, so Sherry's parents sent her from the Midwest to the West Coast to give birth.

Later Sherry and Steve married and reared a family together, never telling their children, their friends, or the members of the church Steve pastored about the baby they had given up for adoption. When Beth learned their identities and nervously made that life-changing phone call to them, all of that changed. They quickly welcomed her into their family back in the Midwest and later introduced her to their church.

Shortly after Beth and Sherry became acquainted, they went together to the facility in Los Angeles where Sherry had stayed during her teenage pregnancy and where she gave birth to Beth. Just as I was terrified by a forgotten memory when Ken and I revisited Lonely Acres, Beth was similarly affected when a buried memory came crashing down on her there.

I've asked Beth to share a portion of that experience with you:

When my birth mother, Sherry, came to California to visit me, we visited the maternity home where she had stayed for the two weeks prior to my birth. During this visit I discovered that when Sherry had been there, twenty-three years prior, the facility also had an attached hospital where the girls would go to give birth. During our tour we took the elevator down to what used to be the hospital, just as Sherry had done in the early morning hours of August 16, 1961.

As we came out of the elevator and were walking down a corridor, I experienced a wave of strong emotions. I became dizzy and lightheaded and had to stop to get my balance. Surprisingly, the emotions I felt were terror and despair; tears sprang up in my eyes. The woman from the maternity home who was giving us the tour noticed I was crying. When I shared what I was experiencing, she told me we were in the corridor I had been wheeled down in an Isolette immediately after birth. I was taken to the nursery where I stayed until going to a foster home to await my adoption.

A second experience of remembering happened a few years ago during a professional training session dealing with trauma. The participants were asked to pair up and practice some therapeutic interventions to help process our own traumas.

During my turn at being the client, I chose to deal with a car accident I had been in on Valentine's Day, which also happened to be the day my husband had asked me for a separation. While describing the picture of me sitting on the curb with the other driver after the accident, both of us unharmed and waiting for the police to arrive, the picture changed.

Suddenly I saw myself curled up in the fetal position on the cold, hard sidewalk. As I continued to describe what I was experiencing, it was clear that my mind was taking me back to the Isolette in that maternity home in LA.

I felt cold, alone, curled up, and utterly abandoned. Again tears sprang to my eyes. My chest felt tight, and my head was swimming with emotions terror and despair that I did not want to relive at that moment.

Wanting it to stop, I was, with the help of the trainer, able to visualize Jesus picking me up off the sidewalk and rocking me in His arms, comforting me and restoring my peace.

For many years I had sensed that dark memories rooted in my earliest moments of life were locked away inside of me. But I avoided fully processing those early memories. They were too scary, too raw. They made me feel so vulnerable and alone. They filled me with the fear that I was not lovable and no one wanted me.

It is no wonder that, thinking back to that Valentine's Day when my husband asked for a separation, I was so quickly transported to my first feelings of abandonment. Not having been held by my birth mother as a newborn but rather having been whisked away to an Isolette had left a wound that did not heal.

A growing pool of research surrounding pre- and post-birth experiences indicates that babies can have emotions and memories rooted in their earliest moments that profoundly affect their feelings about themselves and their place in the world. Based on my own experiences and my own professional studies, I firmly believe this is true.

But I also learned, through my own experiences and professional experiences, that healing of those profoundly hurtful memories can occur. After the trauma workshop, I went back and did some good therapeutic work with that same trainer. That work helped me reprocess those early memories and remember something else: that I was never alone. Jesus has been with me all along and will never leave me or abandon me.

One might expect that Beth's visit to the place where Sherry had stayed and where Beth was born might provoke emotions—but the nondescript hospital corridor? The unexpected image that flashed to Beth's consciousness was of those moments when she had been in that corridor before, and the image unleashed the emotions she had felt when she was there as a newborn. Those feelings had been stored in her memory bank. When they pushed their way to her conscious mind, they were so overwhelming Beth had a strong physical response—dizziness—and an emotional response—tears. Beth pulled herself together to continue with the tour, but afterward she thought, *What was that about?*

Now she knows.

The Mind's Mysterious Storage System

Now, please forgive me for interrupting our discussion, but if you've read any of my books, you know I occasionally lapse into foolishness and insist upon taking a little giggle break. And since we're talking about the crazy way our minds work, it seems appropriate to throw out a bit of crazy silliness now. So, with apologies to all blonde women, I have to share this joke with you that gives me a giggle.

A blonde woman was speeding down the road in her little red sports car and was pulled over by a woman police officer who was also a blonde.

The blonde cop asked to see the blonde's driver's

license. She dug through her purse and was becoming progressively more agitated.

"What does it look like?" she finally asked.

The policewoman replied, "It's square, and it has your picture on it."

The driver finally found a square mirror in her purse, looked at it for a moment, and then handed it to the policewoman. "Here it is," she said.

The blonde officer stared into the mirror, handed it back, and said, "Okay, you can go. I didn't realize you were a cop."

Isn't the mind a marvelous thing? And one of the most amazing things about it, at least in my experience, is that it can suddenly go AWOL without any indication that it was even considering an extracurricular excursion. I love that joke because I frequently have moments when I identify with those two blondes as I sigh to myself, *Marilyn, where is your mind?* The answer is on the corner of my desk where a teacup coaster reads, "My mind not only wanders, it sometimes leaves completely."

In this chapter we're considering the power of abandonment memories to hide away in the secret recesses of our mind. We may have completely forgotten a powerful memory, but nevertheless, it may have an unperceived influence on our lives—our behavior, our thoughts, our attitudes. If we are able to be open about finding the source of these behaviors, thoughts, and attitudes, it might just be that this secret memory can be exposed and examined before it sparks a sudden, surprising event that comes crashing down on us in unexpected ways, provoking unexpected physical and emotional responses. But where, exactly, do those secret memories come crashing down *from*?

Memories are hidden somewhere within the mind, which, as we've just discussed, sometimes has a tendency to play tricks on us. The mind is a part of the brain, which, fortunately, is trapped inside our skull so it can't slip off with our mind when it goes tiptoeing through the tulips in la-la land. There's no easy distinction to be made between the mind and the brain, so I won't try to define one except to say the brain is utterly fascinating and far too complex for my mind to grasp. Research tells us the brain consists of around one hundred billion nerve cells (neurons) that send and receive signals, as well as nearly five thousand billion helper cells that support the activity and survival of the neurons. Somewhere in all that mysterious maze of cell business is my memory. (I knew it had to be somewhere.)

To many of us, memory can be frustrating because it, too, tends to go missing occasionally or (in my case) frequently: "I think I remember buying her a birthday present, but I can't for the life of me remember where I put it. On the other hand, do I really remember buying her a present, or did we just have lunch instead? Now that

I bring up the subject, where did we have lunch if indeed we did, and what did I order?"

Even though specific memories are sometimes hard to summon when we need them, our memories are never banished. They remain in the brain's "memory vault," waiting to be summoned—or perhaps hiding when they *are* summoned.

The mystery and wonder of the mind and its system of storage is another tribute to the God who created us all, as the psalm says, in that "wonderfully complex" fashion. (Ps. 139:14)

Reprocessing Abandonment Memories

Researchers who study memory have yet to fully comprehend its miraculous intricacy. With that in mind, I don't want to reduce the mystery of memory into "Dick and Jane" language. But for the sake of simplicity, I'd like to suggest we see ourselves as little walking, talking photo albums, and that we switch from the metaphor of the memory vault to the memory album.

We go about our lives carrying secret, troubling pictures we don't even know we have—or if we do know we have them, we'd like to throw them away. But since memory doesn't throw *anything* away, we try to forget the troublesome photos. When that happens, the images—the secrets—get pushed down into the unconscious, where the album is protected and safe.

But the fact that those pictures are in the album and that we sometimes receive flashes of them tells us we need to look at them, exclaim over them, and perhaps cry over them. When we acknowledge the hurt, pain, confusion, or embarrassment they may produce, our next step is to show them to the Father who, incidentally, already sees them, and then to ask His help in processing them.

It may also be helpful for us to seek out a trained professional who can help us feel safe as we look for, reveal, and *feel* the secret contents of our albums. After experiencing the Lonely Acres flashback with Ken, I put it back in the album—not to be forgotten but with no clue what it meant or how it influenced my behavior. It slipped into the pages of my conscious-mind album under the heading *What was that about?* Later I had a trained professional help me page through my memory album so I could reprocess that abandonment memory, incorporate Jesus into the revised version, and make it easier to live with.

It is incredibly comforting to know God is not indifferent to my lifetime of *What was that about?* experiences. But notice that *He* doesn't ask the question. *I* do. Sometimes I get an answer, and sometimes I simply must rest in what He knows and I may never know. I trust that He has a plan for my life (Jer. 29:11) and that He knows what He's doing. As the Old Testament character Job humbly said to God (after enduring some harsh setbacks and asking, *What was that about?*), "I'm convinced: You can do anything and everything. Nothing and no one can upset your plans" (Job 42:2 MSG).

Reprocessing Memories You Didn't Know You Had

Beth didn't know she had felt abandoned so early in life . . . until the scene flashed before her in the hospital corridor. As a newborn she had seen it and felt it, but then her brain tucked the memory away into her memory vault. Thirty-five years later it reemerged in a strong way, and she sought out a professional's help to process it. With the aid of that empathic professional, Beth reprocessed that memory to eliminate—or at least reduce—its hurtful impact. A secret became known; understanding was gained.

With the psychotherapy trainer providing a safe, re-assuring environment for her to relive the memory, Beth saw herself in all her helplessness and vulnerability as she was rolled away from her first mother in the cold and non-nurturing Isolette. She was heading into nine days of hav-ing her needs attended to by a competent but overworked staff in an environment completely unlike the warmth and safety of the womb she had so recently left behind.

As she reprocessed this image, instead of seeing herself alone in the nursery, attended to but not loved, Beth saw Jesus smiling over her Isolette. She saw Him as described in Zephaniah 3:17: "He will take great delight in you, he will quiet you with his love, he will rejoice over you with singing" (NIV).

Abandonment memories can be harsh and hurtful. But the pain they inflict is soothed when we see, instead, the Creator of the world *singing* over us and taking great delight in us. There is great relief in seeing ourselves held in His arms, our faces nestled into His neck.

An unperceived buried memory of abandonment may be a "secret" hidden within us that causes us to feel emotional pain we can't understand—until that memory is brought into the light of God's healing. Often we need a trained professional to help us identify and process how it got there. Throughout that process we can be confident that the ultimate solution for both the question and the pain of abandonment is found in God's promises to always be with us. Of those many promises, here's my favorite. If you've seen my hair, you'll know why this one speaks especially to me:

> I have cared for you before you were born. . . . I will be
> your God throughout your lifetime—until your hair is

white with age. I made you, and I will care for you. I
will carry you along and save you. (Isa. 46:3–4)

·············
Keep Talking
·············

1. Have you ever experienced unexpected and unexplained
   feelings that have suddenly enveloped you during a visit
   to a place, or even a person, related to an earlier time
   in your life?

2. In light of the stories shared in this chapter, can you
   now consider those feelings in a new way, understand-
   ing what might have sparked them?

3. If you're able to gain understanding from that incident,
   can you see how that memory may have been linked to a
   secret fear, perhaps a fear of abandonment or some
   other emotional issue? How has its impact manifested
   itself in your everyday life?

4. Knowing that such memories are never lost but are
   stored away in your memory vault, how can you prevent
   future life storms and challenging events from settling
   in as powerful secrets hidden away in your psyche?

FIVE

Secret Pleasures, Addictions, and Thoughts

What is your idea of pleasure? I recently asked that question of a number of my friends, all of whom are basically sane and stable. The answer I received the most frequently was to sink into a warm, relaxing bubble bath with a great book and a Do Not Disturb sign on the door.

Though I think the idea is pleasant, for me, the challenge of keeping my book dry and the water temperature constant is too troubling to be worth the effort. I prefer a warm shower. I'll read when I dry off.

I got a giggle reading about a unique bath invented in 1636 by an Italian, Doctor Sanctorius. It was called the "bath bag." The bather crawled into a large leather sack and had the top of the bag sealed around the neck like a collar. Hot water was then poured in through a funnel at the bather's shoulder. It washed over the body and down toward the feet where it drained out of a long spout. If the bather preferred a leisurely soak, the spout could be plugged. Certain models had watertight arms and gloves enabling one to read or write while enjoying a continuous cleansing flow.

Dr. Sanctorius believed the principle advantage of his bath bag was that it allowed the bather to receive visitors while still maintaining modesty and decency. This solution for ridding the body of a day's worth of dirt and tension strikes me as a bit harebrained. However, the idea of watertight arms and gloves has possibilities. But of course the problem of water temperature maintenance would still exist. Maybe one of the "visitors" could see to that.

Pleasure is one of God's gifts. Even so, from the Puritans to the Amish, Christians have historically felt a certain distrust of pleasure. There are some seemingly crabby verses that could support that distrust. Second Timothy 3:4 warns us not to love pleasure more than God. A few others:

> But the widow who lives for pleasure is dead even while she lives. (I Tim. 5:6 NIV)

> Traitors, heady, highminded, lovers of pleasure more than lovers of God. (2 Tim. 3:4 KJV)

> You pleasure-loving kingdom, living at ease and feeling secure. (Isa. 47:8)

If taken out of context, these verses might make us doubt that pleasure is one of God's gifts. How could it be? It sounds as if pleasure and trouble go together. A friend of mine told me she was raised in a very strict and unforgiving faith culture that said, "If you're smiling, you must be having fun. If you're having fun, you must be sinning. So don't smile!" That thinking implies smiling is the first step toward total moral collapse.

As in all things, we want to maintain a balanced and thoughtful understanding of what the Bible teaches about pleasure. Consider the following verses:

God, who richly gives us all we need for our enjoyment. (1 Tim. 6:17)

Whatever is good and perfect comes to us from God. (James 1:17)

God intends that His good and perfect creation will be appreciated by us; that it give us pleasure. I love that after each of God's creative acts recorded in Genesis, He stood back and "saw that it was good" (Gen. 1:10). He encourages us to see just how good! Seeing the grandeur of His creation gives me enormous pleasure. Edith Schaeffer described the incomparable handiwork of nature as "Eden's leftover beauty." It is there for us to enjoy; it is something from which we are to derive pleasure. Give me a cup of tea and a comfortable chair, and my pleasure from "leftover beauty" has no limit. It is a sweet way to worship the God who reminds me, "In [My] presence is fullness of joy; at [My] right hand are pleasures forevermore" (Ps. 16:11 NKJV).

Obviously Scripture is not telling us to avoid pleasure; it can be a call to worship. It does, however, encourage us to experience pleasure with disciplined common sense. It makes sense that we strive for balance in all we do. It's possible to exercise too much, diet too much, talk too much, talk too little, discipline too much, discipline too little, volunteer too much, volunteer too little, drive too fast, drive too slow . . . you get the point. For many people, the challenge is to keep pleasure in a state of balance. When a pleasure takes control of our lives, problems occur; dark secrets are created.

Craving More, Creating Secrets

There is a portion of the human brain scientists refer to as the "pleasure center." It is a part of the brain that reacts enthusiastically to chocolate, pizza, pasta, lemon meringue pie, and any other favorite food or activity that provides pleasure. But we need to keep an eye on the pleasure center because it also loves the concept of "more." And the truth is that the "more is better" lie was concocted by the enemy of the soul. "More" keeps us craving and not satisfied. The enemy baits the hook with "more," dangles it in front of the pleasure center, and then waits for us to swallow it. If we do so, we can lose our balance. The result can produce behavior that invokes shame—and causes us to create the dark secrets we hope no one else will discover about us.

For example, when sitting alone at home on a weekend evening, one or two chocolate butter-cream truffles may seem like reasonable "companions." Then the "more" hook swings by, and perhaps several more chocolate butter-cream truffles also seem reasonable—until the box is consumed and we feel nauseous as well as guilty. Are we doomed to forever devour multiple chocolate butter-creams because we swallowed the hook that one lonely Friday night? No, but we'd better sit up and take notice of that hook because it never tires of dangling luring enticements. The lure may change, but the false promise that more is better will *not* change. That lie can apply itself to anything in our lives.

Here's the sobering truth about the pleasure center: It is where the enemy hangs out. It's where the bait is stored and the hooks are sharpened. That does not make the pleasure center evil; it reminds us the enemy will take good and turn it into evil if given the opportunity. There was nothing evil about Eden's apple. It became an instrument of evil because God forbade eating it. Disobeying God was the baited hook, not the apple.

Here's one of the ways the enemy subverts our God-given pleasure center with the "more" hook: we love to be thrilled! There is a certain "high" that comes with being thrilled. We love to watch death-defying trapeze artists, a championship football game tied with ten seconds to go, souped-up race cars zooming at 150 miles an hour, or an Olympic swim competition where the American wins by a fingernail. Those are perfectly legitimate highs. We can, however, become addicted to thrills. Why? Because thrills produce a high. The high itself is not evil, but the "more" search can lead to evil. Proverbs 21:17 from *The Message* states, "You're addicted to thrills? What an empty life! The pursuit of pleasure is never satisfied."

The enemy knows that the pleasure pursuit is never satisfied. That's why, if we are not vigilant, his "more" hook will work. He also knows the "more" pursuit can produce addictions. And those addictions create the dark secrets that can wreak havoc with our happiness. It can be a heartbreaking cycle, one in which balance can be tragically lost and lives can be devastated.

Let's take a minute to consider just what happens in the pleasure center that produces the much-sought-after high. There are two key neurotransmitters in the brain: endorphins and dopamine. Those secretions have much the same molecular structure as morphine. When a substance (drugs, alcohol, or any other addictive stimulation) connects with the pleasure center, toots and whistles go off! Stimulation of the center causes the receptors on the neurotransmitters of brain cells to multiply. So when the addictive substance wears off, the newly created receptions need more. If they don't get more, the pleasure center is out of balance because more of the addictive substance is needed to produce the same high. That "more," if not satisfied, creates cravings.

Cravings require the pleasure seeker to find new and different ways to increase the brain's production levels of dopamine or endorphins. For the emerging alcoholic, that may mean switching from beer to wine and wine to hard liquor. In the case of the drug user, it may mean switching from marijuana to cocaine, coke to crack or methamphetamines.

So how does one know if he or she is addicted? Addiction is not only craving more, it is devoting oneself habitually and compulsively to getting it. That means the addicted person's world revolves around one pursuit only: getting high and maintaining it. He or she reaches the point of caring only for the high and nothing else. This addictive pursuit of more usually sinks into destructive secrecy, where it may continue for years until exposed by calamity— or treated after help is sought and secrets are shared.

A Family Full of Secrets

I'll never forget the look on her face as she sat in my office saying, "I've lost everything . . . my marriage, my children, my friends, and, I'm sure, God as well." She was still a pretty lady at age fifty-one, but the effects of her alcoholism showed on her slightly mottled skin and in her faded blue eyes. Her husband had pastored a number of churches, always managing to stay ahead of the rumors that his wife frequently appeared inebriated at church functions. Her two children did not bring friends home from school, because she was usually passed out on the couch by three o'clock in the afternoon.

After the two boys went off to college, her husband, weighted down by her inability to function, resigned from the church, filed for divorce, and moved to another state.

"They all did what they could," she said, "but I've been what you call down-and-out for ten years." She was a court-appointed client of mine. To avoid jail time, the judge demanded she enroll in a twelve-step program as well as attend weekly counseling sessions with me.

I knew the judge's wife and suspected she was personally paying for the counseling as well as facilitating the woman's attendance at AA meetings. A recovering alcoholic herself and a committed believer in Christ, the judge's wife was determined that her years of alcoholism would serve a redemptive purpose in the lives of those God placed in her path. My new client was hopefully on that redemptive path.

Before we continue, let's attempt to find an answer to explain why a person reaches the point of caring only for the high and nothing else. There are a number of factors to take into account in answering that question, but the bottom line is that they don't care. They don't care enough for their spouse, children, or friends to admit their addictions and seek help. They don't care enough that they have lost their reputation and the loving support of others. They don't care even when their worlds collapse. They have reached the point of caring only for feeding their cravings and maintaining their highs. Usually at this point, they think they are submitting to their cravings in secrecy; the truth is, the origin of the secret may still be hidden, but the once-secret behavior is by now public knowledge.

How does anyone come to the place of losing everything without even caring? How can that be? This totally out-of-balance pleasure seeker cared at one time, but that is the tragedy of sliding from balanced pleasure to totally out-of-balance pleasure. Everything, including caring about anything, is lost in the search for the preferred and new necessary high.

Here's an important fact that can help us understand

the secret source of destructive behaviors: *addiction of any kind serves a crucial function—it distracts from pain*. All addiction is about distracting the user from feeling pain. That pain may be current or buried deeply beyond conscious knowledge, but pain drives the addiction. The victim thinks, *Those feelings are so overwhelming, threatening, and persistent, I cannot cope with them.*

At this point, the ever-watchful enemy baits the hook that says, "You don't have to cope with that pain. Here, try this . . . use this . . . you will feel better immediately. No one has to know. A little bit won't hurt."

Those who swallow the bait are hooked into a distraction that produces the feeling, *I no longer care*.

The best thing that could have happened to my new client was that her secret was exposed—twice, each time with devastating consequences. The first time, she lost her marriage, family, and reputation, but that brought about the second catastrophic exposure, which ultimately led to her rescue.

Her husband left her with a car as well as a small apartment for which he paid the monthly rent. When my client hit a child on his bicycle and was arrested for drunk driving, her secret was revealed again, and the second devastation joined the rubble of the first one. It was then she decided to make a choice. "I can continue not to care and live with the consequences of that choice, or I can decide I want to get well. To get well I have to admit my life is totally unmanageable."

Alcoholics Anonymous (AA) believes it is easier to help alcoholics when they "hit bottom," or with our metaphor, when the roof caves in. It's then that their lives are so shattered and broken they are forced to make a choice to work through the pain of what caused the addiction. Was there a solution for my client? Absolutely. God had never removed His hand from her life or His love from her soul. But it was a long, hard journey for her, and the work was slow and sometimes agonizing.

Seeking Out Secrets and Healing Vulnerabilities

I am an ardent supporter of twelve-step programs that insist on personal accountability and group encouragement. I am also an ardent supporter of counseling, a procedure one seeks out for increased understanding of why and how the pleasure center got so destructively out of balance and the secrets settled in.

Counseling is also a place to learn why there was a particular vulnerability for the personally baited hook the enemy knew to dangle in front of his victim. Often this vulnerability may be traced to earlier dark secrets that were planted, knowingly or unconsciously, in the mind.

Understanding the source, or the secrets, behind this predisposed condition can give clarity, but it cannot heal. Only God can heal. As one acquainted with and trained for the challenges presented by emotional imbalance, I have to agree with Psalm 140:7 that the sovereign Lord alone is our deliverer. Mental health workers provide an invaluable service in sorting our secrets and exposing the splinters of vulnerability that fester into addiction. But almighty God does more than provide a service. Isaiah 43:11 dogmatically states, "I, even I, am the LORD, and apart from me there is no savior" (NIV).

My alcoholic client came to realize that God had never left her and never condemned her. It was that tender hard-core truth that daily enabled her to persevere on her redemptive path and determine that she was worth "fixing." She also had to realize that healing is a lifelong journey, not a one-time event. That is a tough reality to accept.

Watching for the Enemy's Secret Hook

So what are we saying in this chapter? God created us to experience pleasure that is found in Him and authored by Him. The enemy, ever at odds with God, is committed to the task of distorting the pleasure center by making it a never-ending source of lies and deception. His goal? The physical, moral, and spiritual destruction of every one of God's people. His method? The baited hook promising "more is better." When we take the hook and swallow the bait, we inevitably lose our balance, and soon we are controlled by the dark secrets we desperately try to hide from those around us.

What are we to do to maintain our balance? Be vigilant as we enjoy the pleasure center and be reminded:

> Give all your worries and cares to God, for he cares about what happens to you. Be careful! Watch out for attacks from the Devil, your great enemy. He prowls around like a roaring lion, looking for some victim to devour. Take a firm stand against him, and be strong in your faith. (1 Peter 5:7–9)

. . . .
Keep Talking
. . . .

1. In what ways do you maintain a balance between the experience of God-created pleasure and disciplined common sense?

2. How do you apply Proverbs 21:17 to your desire to live a balanced life: "You're addicted to thrills? What

an empty life! The pursuit of pleasure is never satisfied" (MSG).

3. How does the enemy of your soul use the lie "more is better" to throw you out of balance?

4. What is the major attraction of addiction? It serves a purpose—what is that purpose?

5. What do you understand about your "pleasure center" located in the brain? Is it necessary to understand it? Why?

····

SIX

····

Where Is God
in My Dark Secrets?

We've talked about the workings of the brain's pleasure center, and we've discussed how, if we swallow the enemy's more-is-better hook, our lives can slip into addiction that creates, or may be rooted in, dark secrets we desperately hide from view.

But addiction is not the only result of a pleasure center that is out of whack. Some destructive behaviors are centered, not in cravings for more, but in secret yearnings that will not go away and hidden longings that cannot be satisfied. Where is God when we need Him to change the secret feelings that swirl within us, threatening to wreak havoc if we give in to them? Such questions were brought up in this letter:

Dear Marilyn,

I am forty-one years old (yikes) and have never been married. My desire to have a husband is stronger than any other desire I have ever had. My longing to be intimate with a man is very strong. But the Lord hasn't sent the right man my way—yet.

I do not believe that I was created to live alone for the rest of my life, yet I am alone. The Lord has created within me very strong sexual desires that I have not been successful in keeping in check. I have failed miserably in that arena. However, the Lord has not taken those desires away from me.

Is this a test? Am I supposed to be "perfectly" obedient before He will reward me? Am I supposed to remain single the rest of my miserable life? Or is it just "not my time yet"?

I have been asking these questions of the Lord for years. I don't think there really is an answer to this.

—Miserable

What *are* we supposed to do with secret yearnings that will not go away and hidden longings that cannot be satisfied? Where is God in it all? These are understandable and common questions, yet the answer is simple. The problem is that many of us don't like the answer.

So what *is* the answer? God is sovereign, which means He rules. Psalm 115:3 says, "For our God is in the heavens, and he does as he wishes." Jeremiah 10:23 says, "I know, LORD, that a person's life is not his own. No one is able to plan his own course."

You say, "I do not believe that I was created to live alone for the rest of my life." How do you *know* that? You are assuming that because you want to be married, it must be God's plan for you to be married. Baby, it might not be God's plan for you to marry. That isn't a cruel action on God's part. It is, at least for now, a sovereign action on His part. The crucial question is, of course, are you willing to accept His sovereign action?

You say, "The Lord has created within me very strong sexual desires." Then you anonymously share your secret: you have not been successful in "keeping them in check" and you have "failed miserably in that arena." And then, as if you're blaming God for your indiscretions, you say, "The Lord has not taken those desires away from me."

You've taken an important step by actually acknowledging the secret you have probably held hidden away for a long time: you've been promiscuous. Now is the time to present your body to God as a living sacrifice.

You are not your own; you've been bought with a price. I know this sounds cranky, but you are called to purity whether or not it interferes with your secret desires. When you live outside the God-ordained place of purity, you invite many sin complications: disease, pregnancy, affairs, and so forth. Those are sobering possible consequences.

Were any of those consequences to enter your world, blaming God because He didn't take away your sex drive would not be an option. You would need to take full responsibility for those consequences yourself. The Bible is not an optional guidebook. We, His creation, are to obey it.

"Am I supposed to remain single the rest of my miserable life?" Misery is a choice. God in His sovereign design for your life does not will you to misery. He wills for you to show obedience to His Word and peace as you do what's best for your life.

In contrast to the preceding question, consider this desperate plea of a woman who is secretly longing to be released from her marriage vow.

> Dear Marilyn,
>
> I thought I wanted to be married more than anything in life. I've been married for ten years. I'm bored, unfulfilled, and sure this marriage is not God's plan for my abundant life. I know God has a better plan for me. I missed it by marrying too soon. I can't believe a loving God would make me stick this out for the rest of my life.
>
> —Trapped

I began this chapter by asking, "What do we do with secret yearnings and hidden longings that can't be satisfied and won't go away?" It seems wise to always examine our feelings and yearnings. In doing that we ask a few questions about these longings: are they reasonable, are they realistic, and are they morally acceptable? From there we decide if our thinking needs to be transformed. Again, the first step is in carefully sharing the secret yearnings that, in this case, threaten to break apart a ten-year marriage. Perhaps as we gently probe the root of the feelings we can shed enlightenment and understanding that will, with God's help, bring resolution.

To begin, Trapped, let me ask some quick questions about your secret longing to be free from your husband. Then I'll suggest some equally quick, instinctive (on my part, based on my professional training and my Christian beliefs) answers.

Is your longing reasonable? Yes, I would say it is reasonable. You're bored.

Is your longing realistic? Probably not—few experiences in life measure up to our expectations.

Is your longing morally acceptable? According to the world's standard, it is; according to God's standard, it is not.

It sounds as if the question we really need to talk about is the "morally acceptable" one. Unless your husband is an adulterer, you do not have biblical grounds for divorce. That being the case, let's consider your boredom.

What aspect of your marriage is boring? Is your husband a bore? Does he know how to communicate his thoughts and feelings? Are his thoughts and feelings duller than dirt? In other words, figure out what's boring you. Also, do you have a pattern of being bored? Did you wander off in your mind while your English teacher explained the fascinating process of diagramming a sentence or the value of antecedents? If you hung on every word of all that, then you must be married to the world's dullest man! (Just a touch of humor.)

Actually, baby, my hunch is that you have a pattern of feeling bored in other arenas of your life as well. While you're thinking that through, take the initiative to break the boredom cycle. What can you do to make your marriage more interesting? If the marriage is boring to you, chances are it's boring to your husband as well. Figure out a few fun things to do together. Ever try bowling? I took my grandchildren bowling a few months ago. I had not bowled in thirty years. As I lined up my ball with the pins and stepped adroitly down the lane to throw the ball, it would not let go of my thumb. The ball and I went hurtling down the lane together. Ian, my grandson, never recovered. He laughed helplessly all evening. My swollen thumb was worth the price of seeing Ian sprawled in a fit of laughter over my efforts to free my hand.

My point is, sometimes it doesn't take a lot to perk things up. Think about it, talk about it, and then do something about it.

And remember that God is sovereign. You didn't miss His plan. You may not like the plan, but God does what He does. I can fuss, but in the end it is His will that is accomplished. Ephesians 1:11 says, "He makes everything work out according to his plan."

Does that mean we're all little robots with no will of our own? No, we are not little robots. I have yet to figure out how my will is figured into the sovereign equation of my life experience. But it is comforting to know my life is not a random shot propelled by either my bad choices or my good choices. God makes good of my bad choices as well. That's His promise. The profound truth of the sometimes glibly quoted Romans 8:28 is a huge comfort to those of us who regret, worry, and blame ourselves for "missing the plan." I suggest to you, dear one, that God will bring good out of the marriage you're secretly dying to get out of. I'd also suggest you may come to love the plan!

In the meantime, memorize Romans 8:28; it's definitely not boring! "And we know that God causes everything to work together for the good of those who love God and are called according to his purpose for them."

The Secret Longings and Frustrations of Parenthood

We'll move off the subject of marriage with its powerful longings and onto the subject of parenting. It, too, has secret longings and many frustrations.

Dear Marilyn,

How should a mother relate to a child who is obviously living a sinful life—drugs, irresponsibility, sexual promiscuity, etc.? Shun, act as if everything is okay, give them money when they can't pay bills? By the way, where's God?

—Heartbroken

Actually, this question and its answer are for anyone trying to deal with someone you love whose life is out of control from "sinful living." Some of you are desperately trying to keep your children's behaviors secret so that your role as a godly Christlike leader won't be tarnished. I hope you will recall, and be encouraged by, my earlier story about the pastor's wife who confided that she was tired of wearing a mask of secrecy about her struggles with bulimia. And I hope the preceding discussion on God's sovereignty will be helpful to you as we consider some possible solutions for your child's behavior. We know that God never wills sin or tempts us to sin. We seem to manage that quite well on our own. God gets no blame for what we choose. We want to harbor in God's sovereignty and the sure knowledge that He will bring good out of life's "bad." In so doing, we will be made stronger and more aware of His provision. I believe it is possible to rest in Him, because we can trust in Him to be the God of everything.

Having reminded ourselves of this great harboring for our souls, and remembering the importance of finding a trusted person with whom you might confide this dark secret and gain help in easing its impact on *you*, let's discuss a few practicalities for dealing with your child's situation.

First, do not give your child money. Pay the food bill, the clothing bill, and any school bills yourself. Otherwise, whatever money your child receives will undoubtedly be used for drugs and the like. Even though that does not mean the money supply will dry up, it does mean you will not be contributing to it.

Do not shun your child, but by the same token, do not accept unacceptable behavior. Set boundaries, and don't change them. Decide what is not tolerable behavior, and communicate that with your child. Don't waver. Stay firm and be consistent. Join a twelve-step group that brings parents with the same kinds of kid issues together to support one another. There you will bring your secret into the light; do not pretend you don't know what's going on. You do know, so say so. In saying so, make it clear what kind of discipline you will use and when you will use it.

And even as you maintain disciplinary standards, you need to communicate caring and love. When children are in a world of secret hurts, they usually show it through negative and often self-destructive behavior.

Now to my real concern: what is going on in the life of this child? Consider what dark secrets might be the source of his or her problem. Generally, this kind of behavior comes from acting out negative feelings rather than verbally expressing them. Have there been any major changes in your environment that may have thrown this kid out of balance? Are problems in your marriage producing fights and other disruptions? Has there been a move—new school, new neighborhood, loss of old friends? Might there be a school challenge you know nothing about—bullying or rejection? Are the grades slipping? Have you met with the teachers or the principal? Something's going on beyond the usual teen rebellion. Learn all you can.

Finally, you deserve to have a professional walk this path with you. Find a therapist who specializes in troubled teens or young adults. That professional will have local referrals in the event you need emergency care for your child. Please do not shrug off your own need for support. Buried secrets about your child's unacceptable behavior can infect your life as viciously as they do your child's.

Bring them into the light, let someone help you sort them out, and then ask God to help you heal from their impact on you.

Now that we've discussed the practical response, let's address your question, "By the way, where's God?" one more time. Though you may not feel Him or sense Him, God is right by your side. That's His promise to you and to your child. Remember, He is sovereignly orchestrating the details of your life in spite of appearances.

And also consider this: while you're wrestling with your dark secrets and asking, where is God? He may also be asking the same about *you*.

Why God Asks, "Where Are You?"

To help you understand what I mean when I suggest that God may be asking as to your whereabouts, let's do a quick replay of the post-apple scene in the garden. Because Adam and Eve had eaten of the tree of the knowledge of good and evil, they knew they had done a "bad thing." Genesis 3:8–9 describes their shame: "Toward evening they heard the LORD God walking about in the garden, so they hid themselves among the trees. The LORD God called to Adam, 'Where are you?'"

The point here is not their hiding in shame; we all do

that when we've done a bad thing. The point here is that *God came looking for them*; He sought them out with the question, "Where are you?"

God didn't ask the question because He didn't know where they were. He asked the question so that they might *admit* where they were. He also asked the question so they could choose to respond to Him—or try to avoid Him by remaining hidden. They chose to come out of hiding.

When they did so, God did the most amazingly nurturing thing: "And the LORD God made clothing from animal skins for Adam and his wife" (v. 21). They had not known shame before they disobeyed, but having done so, they needed clothes.

God seeks us out, even when we've made bad choices. When we open ourselves to him, when we share our darkest "secrets," He does not leave us to sink deeper and deeper into our chosen messes. Instead, He comes after us, shining His heavenly light on those secrets hiding in the dark corners of our hearts, and asking for our response to the question, "Where are you?" He does not ever sever the inseparable bonds He wraps around us.

In my heart, I believe God never leaves us. Yet there was a time in my life when I briefly shared this woman's poignant feeling of heavenly abandonment. I, too, wondered, *Where is God?*

That question became personal to my life as I saw my

mother grapple with the loss of His presence. For her, the familiar cry, "Where is God?" gave way to the disillusioned whisper, "He is gone."

My mom was my priest. She taught me Scripture. She taught me moral and ethical principles, and she introduced me to Jesus when I was five years old. I always knew she was not God, but she seemed like it much of the time. I confused her with God because she was patient, long-suffering, and gentle. She never raised her voice; I always felt her love.

Though she was far more seriously inclined than I, she loved to laugh, and there were many times we literally fell into a heap laughing together. During a tour of John Knox's house in Edinburgh, Scotland, we both got giggly over the guide who droned his way through all the rooms of the house explaining its distinctive architectural features with zero personality. The only animation he exhibited was an unmistakable ocular tic that would occasionally punctuate the ends of his sentences. I was finding his tic a distraction, but because I was hard up for entertainment, I fought valiantly against an inappropriate desire to giggle. Apparently my mother was struggling with the same impulse. When I heard the muffled little snort stuffed deeply in her throat, I couldn't control myself. I let out my unattractive hoot-laugh—and it was all over for both of us. We were formally asked to leave. We leaned against the side of John

Knox's house and together experienced the healing power of laughter. (Inappropriate laughter provides more healing than the socially acceptable kind. Trust me on this.)

My mother was raised in a highly educated environment where "doing good things" was stressed and contributing to the betterment of society was a personal commitment. The Bible was considered to be no more than a collection of aphorisms and occasional bits of good poetry. During the completion of Mom's graduate work in Berkeley, she came to know not only that God loved her but that He sent His Son, Jesus, to provide salvation for her. Her decision to receive Jesus into her heart and mind became the defining moment of her entire life. Mom was an intellectual, so to receive Jesus into her heart as well as her mind was a monumental change for her thinking.

She went to Nyack College and Seminary in New York so that she might learn more about the Bible. In so doing, she met my father. He felt called to the ministry, and together they forged out a philosophy of their life's work. My mother believed whether one has a PhD or a grade-school diploma, human need is the same. It's the same in sophisticated cities; it's the same in rural communities. All people are broken in one way or another, and all people need to be directed to the Great Physician. My parents married and spent a lifetime sharing that ministry.

My mother taught me about prayer. I learned from

her words, but I learned even more by her example. There was something about Mom's quiet dignity that somehow coupled with God's majesty. I know that sounds a bit lofty, but I don't know how else to describe what I observed as well as experienced. When Mom retreated into "her room" and prayed, somehow change came about. Dad, the pastor, was out there making it happen, but Mom was "in there" praying it to happen. Their different approaches for achieving the same goal fascinated me. They seemed to work in harmony.

When I was a sophomore at Seattle Pacific University, my roommate, Karen Petersen, reminded me of my mother. Karen was extremely bright, gentle, loving, and patient, with a fascinating prayer life. Karen and I, like Mom and I, had frequent deep conversations, many of which were about prayer. I was stunned to learn that Karen believed in speaking in tongues. Her mother was an Assembly of God pastor, and a more compelling and tender witness for Jesus I have never met, except of course, my own mother. Karen and her mother gave tremendous credibility to a practice I thought was weird and my father had warned me against when I left for college.

During Christmas break from Seattle Pacific I had my first opportunity to run those speaking-in-tongues thoughts past my mother. I told her how much I admired Karen, how spiritually in touch she seemed, and how responsive I was to Karen's mother. Finally I asked Mom, "What do you think of the whole *tongues* thing?"

Quietly, as always, she said, "Well, Marilyn, it's been my practice for over thirty years."

I looked at her in total disbelief. Falteringly I asked, "Does Daddy know?"

Her response—"He doesn't seem to"—sent me into an hour-long wall stare.

So that explained it. I didn't fully understand it then and I don't fully understand it now, but there was a dose of spiritual high octane in my mother that I relied on and thanked God for; so did my father. I had always been a bit in awe of my mother's intellect, but then I was even more in awe over her spiritual experience and how it evidenced itself in her life. She lived out that spiritual depth in her daily life but withheld some of the specifics from those around her. I wonder now how I would have responded had I known her secret during my growing-up years.

With this bit of history, you can understand then how incomprehensible it was for me several years later as I witnessed my mother's "dark night of the soul" when, in agony, she revealed, by a horrific choice, the secret pain and torment she had been keeping to herself.

She was seventy-two when the headaches began. They were accompanied by excruciating pain in her left arm. The arm pain jumped around, but the headaches stayed put. The normal activities of life—eating, sleeping, walking, thinking—had all become functions that were sometimes beyond her ability.

The doctors couldn't agree on a diagnosis. Had there been a stroke that left nerve damage? Was there a brain tumor causing diminished brain function? Was she just showing signs of aging with symptoms that resisted medication? There were several surgeries, but nothing seemed to help.

I could hardly bear the look of physical anguish I saw in my mother's face. There were several prayer chains that faithfully brought her debilitating pain to the attention of the Great Physician. Many prayed for direct healing; others prayed for her endurance. I prayed that God would be fair. I expected Him to be.

After four years of watching my mother suffer the debilitating headaches and body pain, I began to lose faith in God's system of justice. What Mom was experiencing was not fair; she deserved so much more after her years of loving service to God. He could reverse those pain channels and give her body peace. She could die, but why should she die in such physical devastation? She had been such a saint, not just to me, but to countless others as well.

One morning my father called and said Mom had been rushed to the hospital the night before. She had walked out of her bathroom and handed him an empty bottle. Earlier it had been full of sleeping pills. "I've just swallowed them all," she said.

After having her stomach pumped, she was in a weakened condition, but the doctor said she would recover.

As I frantically drove the two hours from my house to be with her in San Diego, I was aware of a huge shift of new emotions veering over to the edge of my soul. I needed now to be strong, but instead I felt desperate and helpless. Mother had always been my rock. She had always been my mentor, confidant, intercessor, the cushion I slumped into when I felt weak.

I tried yet again to think through how agonizing her life had become. I had watched pain cloud her vision and confuse her thoughts. Her mind, which had been her greatest human asset, had now led her down an unrecognizable path. She had attempted the unthinkable.

I sat next to Mom's hospital bed constantly stroking her hand, her cheek, her hair. She acknowledged me by squeezing my hand occasionally, but otherwise she was silent. Hours later, when I got ready to leave, she opened her eyes, looked at me, and said, "I'm so sorry. I have failed you, your father, and God. Please forgive me."

In a rush of words I assured her she need not ask my forgiveness, that I loved her and would always love her. Her only response was to say, "I don't want anyone to know about this. I'm so embarrassed." At her request, I kept her secret; we never spoke of it again.

So why am I telling it now? Perhaps knowing Mother's story will help you realize there are times when God asks the question, "Where are you?" and, out of shame, you don't respond. You remain hidden. You keep your distress or your failures a secret, embarrassed by what you have done—or perhaps are still doing.

God wants us to feel safe enough to answer, to tell Him the "secrets" He already knows. Why? He wants to maintain our connection. He wants us to feel the inseparable bond that melds Him to us. He wants to assure us that He will work out His plans for our lives.

For my mother, pain was the big disconnector; it seemed to disconnect her from God. She had lost mental clarity as well as spiritual clarity. God knew that and did not judge her; neither did He leave her. I don't think she knew that, though, until He took her to be with Him two months later. She died of pneumonia. Now she knows what she didn't know then.

It's No Secret: God's in Charge

Nothing has been more liberating in my walk with the Lord than understanding and embracing the sovereignty of God. To say God is in charge frees me up to *not* be in charge. I don't know enough to be in charge. Though I will at times mumble about God's plan, I know His way is best for me. When I can't quite figure out what's going on, God can. That is reassuring. It is also reassuring that God invites my participation in what's going on.

We began this chapter by asking where God is as we struggle with the hurtful secrets that sometimes seem to threaten to push us into the dark abyss of despair. Let's conclude by reminding ourselves of the trustworthiness of God's sovereign love through these beautiful words from the Psalms: "Everything God does is right—the trademark on all his works is love" (145:17 MSG).

Where is God when we long for Him to change things, to resolve the secret longings and deep yearnings within us? He's by our side, doing what He does for our well-being and for our growth in Him. He is working "all things according to the counsel of His will" (Eph. 1:11 NKJV). I can rest in that; so can you.

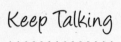

Keep Talking

1. Write a short (or long, for that matter!) letter sharing

a secret that is causing you to question God's presence in your life.

2. When you read back over your letter, picture Jesus sitting with you, listening to you read it aloud. What expression is on His face?

3. Picture Jesus responding to you with His words to the apostles: "Be sure of this: I am with you always, even to the end of the age" (Matt. 28:20). Can you believe Jesus' promise? What "equity" did He provide to assure you His promise is true?

4. What feelings does Jesus' promise to be with you always cause you to have as you consider the dark secrets with which you have struggled? Are you encouraged? Are you comforted?

SEVEN

*Are You Guarding
Your Husband's Secret?*

The secrets that negatively impact our lives may not be exclusively *our* secrets. Remember the mother who shared her secret frustrations and fears related to her wayward son in the previous chapter? Husbands and wives may struggle in similar ways to keep their spouse's secret, shielding him or her by hiding the behavior or addiction so that the family's admirable image may be maintained even though the problem, and the secrecy surrounding it, is in fact destroying the very foundation of that marriage.

This situation can occur when a husband covers for his wife, as described in the example shared earlier of the pastor-husband who helped hide his wife's bulimia. Now, because most of my readers happen to be women, I want to devote this chapter to the reverse situation. The letters shared here repeatedly show the anguish that builds as a wife urgently attempts to hide her husband's dark and destructive secrets. Enabling that secrecy impacts not only the marriage but also the wife's emotional well-being.

In my answers, I hope to assure both the letter-writer and you that healing begins when the destructive secret is shared in a secure environment that abounds with the promise of God's never-failing love and grace.

Dear Marilyn,

Most of my adult life I have been a single mom. I remarried four years ago and try to be a godly wife, allowing my husband to be the spiritual leader of our home. We each had two children from previous marriages and have one together. My husband claims to be a Christian and attends church, but he admits he rarely prays and doesn't read the Bible. His business dealings are often dishonest, and some of his morals, or lack thereof, are being learned and copied by our children.

I have a difficult time keeping quiet about his dishonesty but do so because I do not wish to criticize him in front of our church family. I am starting a new ministry for young adults, and many church leaders are pressuring me to have him be my assistant (he is already a sub for the toddler class).

I try to shield my children from his dishonesty (and usually am successful), but I know that he should not hold a position in the church. Not only are some of his dealings dishonest, but they are illegal. I am torn between my loyalty to my husband and trying to be a godly wife, and my duty to the church in shielding others from his dishonesty. Nobody sees it. He is very popular—the life of the party—and I don't wish to bash him at church. Please, any help would be appreciated.

—Keeping Up Appearances

Okay, darlin', let me be sure I have this straight. You "allow" your husband "to be the spiritual leader" of your home. And you describe his "leadership" in the following ways:

- ⚜ He rarely prays.

- ⚜ He does not read the Bible.

- ⚜ He's dishonest in his business dealings even to the point of breaking the law.

- ⚜ His life is a total sham, and he looks to you to cover for him and make him look good.

You, on the other hand, scramble to divert attention so others do not see who he truly is. And you do this because you want to be a godly wife. Mercy!

I think we need to talk a bit more about wifely submission in marriage. Paul wrote in Colossians 3:18, "Wives, submit to your own husbands, as is fitting in the Lord" (NKJV). The pattern for marriage is that the husband is "fit" to head. He must love his wife as Christ loves the church. He must also love with godly integrity. That means the husband seeks a deeper, closer, and more meaningful relationship with God. From that divine relationship, the husband is equipped to be a leader—a leader a wife can trust.

I'm sorry, baby, but your husband fails on all counts. He is not fit to be the leader of your home. So what does that mean for you, who want to honor him in a position for which he has no qualifications? And what does that say about the degree to which you are to be submissive to him?

Notice the phrase "as is fitting in the Lord." This means that the principle of submission is of the Lord, but it goes beyond that. It means you are not to submit to this husband when he does not follow the Lord. Wives are not under obligation to follow a husband in sin or to quietly condone that sin in the name of marital submission.

You must keep in mind that your first duty is to be submissive not to your husband but to the Lord. Sin can lead a husband to disregard his spiritual role as head. When that happens, you must remember that God has a prior claim on your obedience. Your husband has gone against the divine pattern.

One who refused to submit to her husband's sinful

demand was Queen Vashti. We read her dramatic story in the book of Esther. Her husband, Xerxes, reigned some- time around 486 BC as a Persian king. His sumptuous consumption of all things extravagant is well documented in history. During one of his hugely elaborate parties that went on for days, the king asked his wife, Queen Vashti, to come to the party and dance for the totally drunk men in attendance. Vashti was gorgeous. King Xerxes was licen- tiously proud of her beauty and wanted to show her off. She refused to come. King Xerxes was furious. A woman was never to refuse her husband. But Queen Vashti did. As a result, she was stripped of her title, court approval, and personal freedom. Obviously, Vashti's standard for personal purity came before her desire to be queen or to be submissive to her husband. She stood by a spiritual principle that her husband ignored. I admire her.

I remember the indignation of a husband I once coun- seled. He wanted to use pornography to "spice things up a bit" preceding sex. (Yes, he was a Christian.) The hus- band found the idea exciting; the wife found it offensive. Ultimately, when they couldn't seem to agree, the husband stated, "I'm head of this marriage, and what I say goes!" I was delighted to hear her say, "What goes here is me if you insist on using filth to get yourself revved up for sex."

Perhaps one of the reasons the concept of submis- sion gets such bad press is that women think they have to slavishly submit, even when the head is sick. The slogan "No matter what, you must be submissive to the will of the husband" is not true. That is not God's pattern for marriage. We need never mindlessly follow along with demands that are ungodly.

Let's go back now to Keeping Up Appearances's question of what to do with this fun-loving party boy whom everyone enjoys and no one suspects. I find myself wondering what in the world you, dear one, are doing and why you are doing it. Here's my understanding:

- You continually shield him from church scrutiny, knowing he is dishonest.

- You "shield" his behavior from the children, even though they're beginning to imitate him.

- You are starting a ministry for young adults, and though you're being pressured to use him as an assistant, you "know he should not hold a position in the church."

- You say you are "torn" between your loyalty to your husband, "trying to be a godly wife," and trying to keep the church from finding out he's a crook.

Has it occurred to you that you are participating in his dishonesty? Your efforts to keep everyone from finding out that this man lacks character and integrity enable him to continue his deception. Why are you willing to participate in all these cover-ups? Are you afraid you will end up as a single mom again, only now instead of two children, you'll have five? I certainly agree that singleness may not be a pleasant thought for you, but what price are you willing to pay in your own character and integrity? When all the kids finally get the picture, what kind of example will you be to them? How will you cover that up? What kind of example are you going to be to the young adults you are going to lead and for whom you are to be an example?

If you want God to transform your life by changing the way you think, you have some major rethinking to do. Second Corinthians 6:14 pulls no punches: "Don't team up with those who are unbelievers. How can goodness be a partner with wickedness? How can light live with darkness?" Tend to this soon, sweetheart; you may not have a lot of time.

A Home Torn by Pornography

The following questioner is also struggling with a spouse whose secret sin is affecting their children.

Dear Marilyn,

I fell in love and married the "golden boy" of our small Christian college. He felt God's call to the ministry. I was thrilled to be a pastor's wife.

Five years ago, I discovered his constant use of online pornography. He begged for my support. A part of that support was to keep his dirty secret. He promised to stop; he hasn't. Now I've discovered that our fourteen-year-old son is also doing online porn.

Do I pretend not to know all this? I feel so betrayed. I've lost all respect for my husband, and I'm heartsick his influence may have led to my son's pornography use. I want to run from this. I want a divorce, but what do I do about my son?

—Shocked

Baby, I am so sorry. You must feel as if you've been broadsided by a cement truck. What breaks the heart is not only your husband's deception, but your son's need for immediate help. For that reason, I suggest you not divorce. You may ultimately find your husband's immorality sufficient grounds for divorce, but not yet. Your son needs you, and he requires as much stability in his home environment as you can provide. But first, let's tackle your husband's addiction to pornography.

Your question, "Do I pretend not to know all this?" is

understandable because we all tend to want to deny a problem exists. This difficulty is so enormous that it's hard to know where to begin. We think maybe it will take care of itself and go away. The agony of your husband's situation is that he is a sexual addict. He is addicted to pornography in the same way a drug user is addicted to crack.

The two words we use for the addict are *habitual* and *compulsive*. His habit must be habitually and compulsively fed. The craving is never ending. Your "golden boy" is gripped by an insidious appetite that I'm sure is causing him personal agony and desperation. So what do you do? You cannot ignore it. You cannot hope it will somehow go away by itself. You must join a fight against all that seeks to destroy the two of you. Before we talk about some clinical approaches I recommend, let me first remind you of the spiritual enemy who daily comes against our souls. First Peter 5:8–9 describes him:

> Stay alert! Watch out for your great enemy, the devil. He prowls around like a roaring lion, looking for someone to devour. Stand firm against him, and be strong in your faith.

Satan's greatest tool to use against humankind is sexual perversion and pornography. Its grip is from the pit of hell. So, dear one, you will need to suit up for the battle ahead of you. Psalm 24:8 reminds us whom we are to trust: "The LORD, strong and mighty, the LORD, invincible in battle."

You do not fight without the power of God, and against Him, no one stands. So then, armed with that biblical truth, what do you do?

You must confront your husband with what you know about his Internet pornography patterns. Collect specific data so you can support your findings. Your intent is not to condemn or even accuse. Your intent is to present the facts. In presenting the facts, your husband will have to make some choices.

He may become angry that you have dared to "snoop around" for information that you use against him. He may choose to deny your findings. He may lie and say he only goes on the Internet on rare occasions. He may say pornography is not a problem—every man on occasion reverts to pornography. He may say he only uses pornography because you don't fully satisfy him. That last one is an invitation to either run him over with a lawn mower or lace his coffee with strychnine. I hope you have enough feistiness to be tempted but not to yield to either.

My concern is that you not buy into his weak blame game. His pornography has nothing whatsoever to do with you. It is his sickness, and you did not give it to him.

Be prepared for any number of attempts your husband

may use to avoid taking responsibility for his addiction. Also be prepared to tell him that if he does not face and then address his problem, you will have no choice but to leave him. That is a perfectly legitimate threat for you to use. You may also say his addiction is being played out in the life of your son and that you have no intention of standing by while those you love are being increasingly diseased. After you have presented your facts and made your ultimatum clear, tell him of a number of treatment options you have researched. Insist he agree to treatment.

If your husband chooses to seek help, it is his huge responsibility to come alongside your son and be an example of one who has confessed his sin and now is attempting to grow from and understand his sin. Your husband's example is crucial for your son's healing. He, too, needs to experience one-on-one therapy for his own issue of sexual addiction. You may ultimately all enter into family counseling together. Each family has a unique dynamic that one needs to recognize in its wholeness to understand what happened and why.

And now, dear one, I'll tell you something you probably already know. It would be best for your husband to resign his pastorate. At least in seeking treatment, he can be a good witness of one who is not hiding in the darkness. You will probably endure the isolating judgment of others. Pastors are held to a higher standard, and when they fall, there are some who fall with them, claiming that all Christians are hypocrites. Some will take the opportunity to blame the Christian leader for their own sin. But be strong in the Lord, sweetheart, and remember that "He who is in you is greater than he who is in the world" (1 John 4:4 ESV).

Seeking Help

What are some treatment options for sexual addiction? First, you need to find a therapist who is trained and experienced in treating issues of sexual addiction. My preference for you is that you find someone not only skilled professionally but also knowledgeable about Scripture, the role of the Holy Spirit, and the stand-by-you-always support of God's love. Though a pastor has training for your spiritual need, most pastors are not trained to counsel on the level of sexual addiction.

Next, find a treatment center near you. There are many worthy organizations, and your trained professional can help you connect with one that is suited to your particular situation.

I also strongly recommend twelve-step groups for addicts, though not in place of one-on-one therapy with a professional. Twelve-step groups are great for the support and maintenance of what will be learned in therapy. They are an adjunct to therapy. Again, your mental health professional can help you find one that meets your needs.

. . . .

Keep Talking

. . . .

1. Can you identify with the women whose letters were shared here? How does your situation compare?

2. If you're helping protect your husband's dark secret, what are you doing specifically to help him continue his deception? How does it make you feel to know you're joining him in his dishonesty or immoral behavior?

3. Prepare yourself by researching help groups and then practice what you will say to your husband to confront him about his secret. What specific suggestions will you be prepared to offer him?

4. How does your enabling your husband in his secret affect your children? What will you do *today* to protect them from the effects of his deception? From whom can you seek help outside your family?

EIGHT

Secrets and Sorrows
That Lead to Divorce

A man was leaving a convenience store with his morning coffee when he noticed an unusual funeral procession heading toward the nearby cemetery. A long, black hearse was followed by a second long, black hearse about fifty feet behind. Behind the first and second hearse was a solitary man walking a dog on a leash. Behind him, a short distance back, were about two hundred men walking in single file.

The observer couldn't control his curiosity, so he respectfully approached the man walking the dog and said, "I'm so sorry for your loss. I realize this may be an inappropriate time for me to disturb you, but I've never seen a funeral procession like this. Whose funeral is it?"

"My wife's."

"What happened to her?"

"My dog attacked her."

"But who is in the second hearse?"

"My mother-in-law. She was trying to help my wife when the dog turned on her."

A thoughtful silence between the two men followed. Finally, the observer of it all asked quietly, "Can I borrow the dog?"

The dog's owner replied, "Get in line."

The frustrations of marriage provide endless numbers of jokes about the murderous instincts marriage can inspire. The irrepressible cartoon character Maxine offers her take on the topic: "Men are always whining about how we are suffocating them. Personally, I think if you can hear them whining, you're not pressing hard enough on the pillow."

Why is it that the very relationship that so pleases the heart of God (and the one about which He talks lovingly throughout Scripture) should become the object of very funny but also tasteless jokes? And why is it we recognize that murder is not an option but hope divorce is?

The reason is we want to stop the pain. Our human defense system is wired to react to and put an end to pain. Pain tells us something is wrong and it needs to be fixed. When it's fixed, the smart learner does not repeat that which first produced the pain. The child who touches a hot stove learns to avoid hot stoves in the future. The overeager chef learns to respect a sharp knife when his severed forefinger falls into the salad bowl.

Self-preservation is an instinct. We need to understand and pay attention to that instinct. So then, can one plead, "I have to get a divorce to stop the pain, and if I don't do that, I'll be ignoring my instinct for self-preservation"?

Maybe . . . maybe you do.

Before we discuss the "maybe," let's discuss what kinds of pain drive people to the divorce court. I'll list the most common—and I surely don't have to explain how these issues easily become destructive secrets:

1. Infidelity
2. Abuse—physical, emotional, verbal
3. Addiction—pornography, alcohol, gambling, drugs
4. Incompatibility (irreconcilable differences)

Those who have sincerely placed their lives in the hands of a sovereign God need to know what Scripture teaches about divorce. Is there a "maybe" category? If so, what is it? On the other hand, those who wish to write their own bible can provide their own "maybe" category. The letter-writer back in chapter 6 seemed inclined to add another commandment to the original ten. Her eleventh commandment would read, "Thou shalt not bore!" Based on the breaking of that commandment, she and all other high-maintenance spouses could rush to divorce courts all claiming to be suffering from "spousal fatigue," the inevitable result of boredom.

For those interested in studying the original languages of your self-written bible, the word *bore* can be interpreted "to induce drowsiness, apathy, dull headache, and loss of appetite." The advantage of knowing the linguistic implications of the word *bore* is that *more* people can then rush to the divorce courts. If the judge questions "spousal fatigue" as a justifiable charge, there's the more acceptable "irreconcilable differences" plea based upon the expanded understanding of the linguistic implications of the word *bore*.

So here's the bottom line: unless you write your own bible, "irreconcilable differences"—which may include boredom, drifting apart, multiple unmet needs, loss of respect, and basic incompatibility—does not provide grounds for divorce. It does, however, provide good reason to agree to resurrecting what feels like a dead marriage. How is that done? Stop searching for a divorce "maybe" and begin searching for ways to bring the dead back to life.

Bringing a Dead Marriage Back to Life

My highest recommendation to resuscitate a dead marriage is a good marriage-enrichment or marriage-restoration weekend. The advantage of a weekend is the intense focus on what caused the marriage to get sick in the first place followed by intense focus on how to make it well. This is usually done in small groups whose members come to know each other, support each other, and cheer each other on to new life decisions. All of the group activity is superintended by a licensed counselor trained in ways to inspire insights that will lead the couples to healthy new thinking and behavior. Many couples decide against divorce and reclaim the ways in which their love can be rekindled and grow once again.

There are any number of good marriage-enrichment weekends, but the one I recommend the most highly is New Life Ministries. (Visit www.newlife.com and click on the Get Help link for information and schedules.) I am personally aware of the ways in which that biblically based encounter weekend works and the numbers of marriages that have literally risen from death to life.

After the jump-start a marriage-enrichment weekend provides, I recommend weekly counseling sessions to further facilitate new patterns of relating to each other. This is admittedly not an easy process as you both openly share whatever secrets may have come between you and respond with vulnerability to the counselor's invitation to, "Tell me everything." Successful counseling demands commitment, time, and energy. But it is cheaper and less painful than divorce. It's also God's intent.

So then, speaking of God's intent, and recognizing "irreconcilable differences" is not grounds for divorce, let's talk about the "maybe" category. If you are well churched, you are familiar with the no-divorce-except-for-adultery verses. The bottom-line verse, Malachi 2:16, states that God hates divorce. It goes contrary to everything He intended for His beloved.

To God, marriage is more than a covenant between a man and a woman; it is a mystical union. Jesus described that union in Matthew 19:5–6: "'For this reason a man shall leave his father and mother and be joined to his wife, and the two shall become one flesh . . . they are no longer two, but one flesh. What therefore God has joined together, let no man separate" (NASB). When a man and woman commit to "leave," "cleave," and then consummate their union in the one-flesh act of sexual intercourse, they are joined in a mystical union designed by God.

The Maybe Category

Because humanity could not live a pure life, that mystical union was not always honored, and the maybe category emerged. Jesus said that everyone who divorces his wife, except for the reason of sexual immorality, is wrong (Matt. 19:9). So Jesus is saying when the mystical union is severed by adultery, that severing creates the *maybe* release from the marriage bond. The reason I use the word *maybe* is because many persons hurt by infidelity choose methods designed to bring healing to the pain of betrayal. There again, I recommend the New Life Ministries' weekend session or other equally qualified interventions designed to heal severed relationships.

There is another maybe category for divorce, which we first read about in Exodus 21:10–11. In essence, the book says everyone, even a slave wife, had three rights within marriage: the rights to food, clothing, and love. If these were neglected, the wronged spouse had the right to claim freedom from that marriage. These three rights became the basis of Jewish marriage vows. They were listed on marriage certificates discovered near the Dead Sea. The three provisions of food, clothing, and love were understood literally by the Jews. Each spouse had to provide emotional support for the other.

The foundation for Jewish and Christian marriage is to love, honor, and keep. These vows, together with a vow of sexual faithfulness, have always been the basis for marriage. If these vows promising to provide emotional and physical needs were not honored, according to Old Testament law, divorce was a rightful course of action.

Paul affirmed those marriage stipulations in I Corinthians 7:3–5 when he said married couples owe each other love. He wrote in I Corinthians 7:33–34 that married couples owe each other material support. Paul did not need to say that neglect of these rights was the basis of divorce, because his Jewish audience understood that fact; it was stated on the marriage certificate. So then, anyone who did not receive emotional or physical support could legally seek divorce. (If you wish to further research these ideas, I suggest you read David Instone-Brewer's excellent book *Divorce and Remarriage in the Church*.)

Restoring Emotional Support

So let's talk about some specific instances when emotional support has been jeopardized in marriage. Let's first talk about physical abuse, and by that I mean the bruises, broken bones, blackened eyes kind of abuse. Can we interpret I Corinthians 7 as lending support to those who want to divorce their abusing spouse?

To answer that question, let's consider whether physical abuse severs the marital bond and breaks the vow to "love, honor, and keep." The answer may be obvious, but many of us seek biblical confirmation. We'll begin by studying 1 Corinthians 3:16–17, which emphasizes the sanctity of our bodies that literally serve to house the Spirit of God:

> Don't you realize that all of you together are the temple of God and that the Spirit of God lives in you? God will bring ruin upon anyone who ruins this temple. For God's temple is holy, and you Christians are that temple.

This passage teaches us that when we receive Christ as Savior, the Spirit of God literally enters our interior being, cleanses it from sin, and transforms it into the "temple of God" where He lives the rest of our earthly life. Because God is holy, our bodies become holy; we then are the "keepers" of that holy temple. Using extremely strong language, Scripture says God will "bring ruin upon anyone who ruins this temple." What does that message say to the abuser? Expect ruin. What does it say to the one abused? Take care of the temple!

Taking care of the temple means no longer allowing it to be abused. What does that mean? If divorce does not seem sufficiently scriptural to you, then you need to separate yourself from the "temple-basher." Separating from the abuser means you have laid down a boundary that says, "Stop! You can never abuse this temple again!"

If your boundary is ignored or stepped over, then your abuser must physically leave. If he won't, you must.

When Separating Is Necessary

Scripture has many encouragements for us to separate ourselves from people whose behavior is destructive. Matthew 18:15–17 says we are to tell the offender about his sinful behavior; if that does not work, include several people as backups and present the sinful behavior again. Then take it to the church. If the person still won't turn from the sin, "treat that person as a pagan or a corrupt tax collector" (v. 17).

First Corinthians 5:11 says, "You are not to associate with anyone who claims to be a Christian yet indulges in sexual sin, or is greedy, or worships idols, or is abusive, or a drunkard, or a swindler. Don't even eat with such people." The same message of our need to separate from ungodly behavior is stated in 1 Corinthians 5:13: "You must remove the evil person from among you."

I think separation is also appropriate for the spouse experiencing the betrayal that accompanies certain kinds of addiction. Addictions such as gambling, alcohol, drugs, and pornography are especially demoralizing to a spouse and destabilizing to the home, causing innocent children to feel confused and abandoned. These problems often lead to the secrets that result in enabling behaviors on the part of those innocent loved ones as they desperately struggle to hide their family's brokenness. The impact of these secrets and behaviors can be far-reaching and long-term.

There are times when a tough-love boundary is the only message that registers in the mind of an addict. "I'm leaving or you're leaving. You decide."

God as Husband of the Unfaithful Bride

Let's go back to the God-as-husband model. When God told Abram to leave his home with all its secure familiarity, God made a covenant with Abram that promised a future nation. God and the Hebrew people became husband and wife.

When God first gave the promised land to His bride, He made the terms of their marriage contract clear; it had specific boundaries. We read about them in Deuteronomy 28. Those boundaries were: obey and be blessed or disobey and experience the consequence of being scattered "among all the nations from one end of the earth to the other" (v. 64).

Throughout the Old Testament we see God as the

husband nurturing and protecting His bride, Israel. She, however, was not faithful. She worshiped other gods, rejected His values, and pursued whatever sin she encountered. Because she did not honor her marriage vows and refused to repent, God as husband said He would no longer provide for her needs. The terms of the contract had been broken. He left her to her sin. Jeremiah 3:6–10 says God sent her away and gave her a "writ of divorce" (v. 8 NASB).

So how did the God-as-husband work for the unfaithful wife, Israel? It is still being worked out. God's husband-way is that He knows us, loves us, forgives us, and promises never to leave us. But nothing about the husband-love was passive concerning His rebellious bride. She has paid a heavy price for her centuries of sin choices. Each choice came with consequences. Without repentance and a genuine turning from that sin, the marriage contract is broken. However, there will come a day when repentance and a renewal of vows will restore the marriage relationship between God and His bride.

> "In that coming day," says the LORD, "you will call me 'my husband' instead of 'my master.' . . . I will make you my wife forever, showing you righteousness and justice, unfailing love and compassion. I will be

faithful to you and make you mine, and you will finally know me as Lord." (Hos. 2:16, 19–20)

Following the God-as-husband model, which knows, loves, forgives, and never leaves, is the ideal toward which we frail persons aspire. But abuse and addictions can humiliate and destroy the dignity of the human spirit. They can trample into the ground the struggling, faltering marital love to the point where finally it finds itself in a graveyard with the inscription Never Again. Is it possible to bring that love back from the grave? Yes, but only when genuine repentance occurs and behavior changes; then, and only then, may the embers of that love slowly glow again. I've seen it happen in my work with married couples where abuse and addictions are present. It will happen with God and His bride.

The Necessity of Forgiveness

Let's say you're a wife who has suffered silently and secretly through your husband's abuse or addictions. Now you've opened your heart to someone—I hope a trained professional—who has helped you bring the dark secrets into the light and helped you understand the biblical directives that apply to your situation. At this point, you may choose to leave, maybe divorce, but *you also must choose to forgive*.

Forgiveness does not mean you reestablish the relationship that proved to be death-producing for your marriage. What I'm saying is that a God-enabled forgiveness is necessary to flush out the poison-pool in which unforgiveness languishes. A bitter and unforgiving spirit creates an unhealthy environment for your inner temple where you and God both live. Forgiving frees you to live in interior harmony.

Some of you may not feel God's permission to divorce for any reason other than that of adultery. It may feel as if Scripture is being inappropriately stretched to include the emotional and physical neglect mentioned in Exodus 21:10–11 and affirmed by Paul in 1 Corinthians 7. Jesus was so definitive, and since He did not explicitly state other behaviors allowing for divorce, you may therefore not believe you have biblical grounds.

If indeed you fall into that category, I want to recommend the book *Redemptive Divorce* by Mark W. Gaither. I've never read a more sensitive, biblically balanced, and carefully researched book on marriage and divorce than this. He offers an out-of-the-box way of providing guidance for the suffering partner, healing for the offending spouse, and an amazing catalyst for marital restoration. Mark offers hope for all persons who are feeling they must choose between the lesser of two evils: divorce without sound biblical support or a life of unrelenting misery.

Talk about It

This fact is crucial: however you choose to heal, separate, or divorce, you must not walk that path alone. We are wired for connection. We need a counselor, coach, pastor, or group to encourage our inborn drive for self-preservation. We need to share our secrets with someone and talk about the problems that brought us to that point. Trusted friends or professionals who listen as you share openly can help assure you of your survival, though it seems impossible at times. Take seriously the advice found in Ecclesiastes 4:9–12:

> Two people are better off than one, for they can help each other succeed. If one person falls, the other can reach out and help. But someone who falls alone is in real trouble. Likewise, two people lying close together can keep each other warm. But how can one be warm alone? A person standing alone can be attacked and defeated, but two can stand back-to-back and conquer. Three are even better, for a triple-braided cord is not easily broken.

I also strongly urge you to avoid any and all possible romantic attachments as you walk your recovery path. When the separated or divorced person rebounds into a new relationship, it serves as a welcome distraction from pain, but that distraction also serves as a blinder for understanding what went wrong in the marriage.

We learn from mistakes. We need to know what our mistakes were that may have contributed to the death of the relationship. If we don't know and learn, we'll survive only to repeat the mistakes. That mistake may simply have been an inability to make a wise marital choice. Were there signals you missed during the courtship phase, or did you spot them but naively assume they would disappear after marriage? These are crucial questions for when you need answers.

Now is the time to devote yourself to an understanding of who you were, who you are now, and how you choose to be in the future. It's also a time for emotional and sexual abstinence. Stay with same-sex friends and groups. They can provide a steady, supportive, safe environment during this healing time. Claim the refuge David wrote of in Psalm 32:7: "You are my hiding place; you protect me from trouble. You surround me with songs of victory."

. . . .

Keep Talking

. . . .

1. Why do you think so many people are shocked to find they "fell out of love" at some point after they married?

2. Do you think it is possible to "fall in love" again with the spouse for whom your heart has grown cold? Is there hope for rekindling the spark?

3. If a husband is an abuser, is that grounds for divorce?

4. Does an abused wife have to stay in the marriage when her life and the well-being of her children are in jeopardy? What does Scripture say about that?

5. Why is it important to avoid all romantic involvements during the divorce process?

NINE

Are You Trying to Hide Your Secrets from God?

A passenger in a taxi leaned over to ask the driver a question and tapped him on the shoulder. The driver screamed, lost control of the cab, nearly hit a bus, drove up over the curb, and stopped just inches from a large plate-glass window.

For a few moments everything was silent in the cab, then the still-shaking driver said, "I'm sorry, but you scared me to death."

The frightened passenger apologized to the driver and said he didn't realize a mere tap on the shoulder could scare him so much.

The driver replied, "No, no, I'm sorry. It's entirely my fault. It's just that today is my first day driving a cab . . . I've been driving a hearse for the last twenty-five years."

Sometimes we act as if God might be like that cab-driver. Were we to tell Him our secrets, share with Him how we really feel, He might be so startled and horrified by what we say He'd jump the curb and hit a light pole.

Now, of course we understand in our rational minds that God knows everything we think. *The Message* translation of Psalm 139:2 says, "I'm an open book to you; even from a distance, you know what I'm thinking." Depending on how comfortable we are with being an "open book," we may like the fact we're so thoroughly known, or on the other hand, we may feel busted. A torrent of self-justification may follow the busted realization:

> *Lord, I didn't really think that thought for more than a minute . . . or two.*

> *I didn't really mean any of that stuff about hurting my husband; I think my blood sugar was low.*

> *Well, yes, there are times when I question whether or not You are even hearing me. Of course I know You are, but . . . well . . . it doesn't feel like it. Nothing has changed. It isn't as if I've lost my faith in You . . . It's just You don't seem very present. I know I'll feel better in the morning. Please don't hold these thoughts against me.*

Honest Communication with God

David, writer of the Psalms, did not tiptoe around God out of fear that God would judge him, reject him, or hold his thoughts against him. David whined, fussed, and praised, depending on how he felt and what his circumstances were. He was secure in his relationship with God.

He was also secure in being totally authentic with God. Why? He believed with all his heart that God was committed to him. But David was human, and his faith wobbled when things were going badly. When circumstances were not in his favor, David second-guessed whether God really was committed to him after all. But, unlike many of us, David did not hide his feelings from God. In fact, David modeled for us the kind of honest communication it is possible to have with God, the kind that trusts God to receive our feelings and not judge us for having them.

One of the most startlingly honest psalms is 88. We read it and wonder, *How dare you say that stuff to God! Can you really just come out and tell Him you're begging for help and He seems to be ignoring you? Is it okay to say that many of your prayers feel as if they fall on deaf ears? Isn't talking to God like that disrespectful?*

Let's refresh our memory on this psalm. As you read it, can you imagine feeling safe enough with God to be this real with Him?

> *O Lord, God of my salvation,*
> *I cry out to you by day. I come to you at night.*
> *Now hear my prayer;*
> *listen to my cry.*

For my life is full of troubles,

And death draws near. . . .

I am forgotten,

cut off from your care.

You have thrown me into the lowest pit,

into the darkest depths.

Your anger weighs me down;

with wave after wave you have engulfed me. . . .

My eyes are blinded by my tears.

Each day I beg for your help, O LORD;

I lift my hands to you for mercy. . . .

O LORD, I cry out to you.

I will keep on pleading day by day.

O LORD, why do you reject me?

Why do you turn your face from me?

(Ps. 88:1–3, 5–7, 9, 13–14)

But then David wrote in Psalm 91:1–2, "Those who live in the shelter of the Most High will find rest in the shadow of the Almighty. This I declare of the LORD: He alone is my refuge, my place of safety; he is my God, and I am trusting him."

He expressed his regained peace in Psalm 94:17–18:

Unless the LORD had helped me,

I would soon have settled in the silence of the grave.

I cried out, "I'm slipping!"
But your unfailing love, O LORD, supported me.

David and his emotions were all over the map, and God went all over the map with him. When we are at the end of our rope, God is there with us. He has said, "Never will I leave you; never will I forsake you" (Heb. 13:5 NIV). When our backs are against the wall, God shares the wall with us—not because He has no idea how to bring us out of our distresses, but because He is where we are, and we're at that wall. His purpose will be accomplished in His time and in His way.

Learning to Cry Out
Honestly to God

Some years ago I had a client named Amy whose eighteen-year-old son was hit and killed by a drunk driver. Amy was referred to me by a psychiatrist who wisely put her on an antidepressant medication. Since she was a Christian, he thought I could help her.

When I invited her to "Tell me everything," she told me she had totally lost her enthusiasm for life. Her son, Stan, was all she had. She had been divorced early in the marriage, she had no other children, and both her parents had died of cancer sometime earlier. Humanly speaking, she truly was alone.

After a few sessions, I asked her to talk to me about her view of God and how she talked to Him about Stan's death. At first she looked a little frightened, but then she assured me she had faith in God; she knew Stan was with Him, and one day they would be together.

I asked her again to describe how she talked to God. She said though she still believed in Him, she wasn't talking to Him. She didn't know what to say if she did talk to Him. She also was afraid that if she ever got started talking, she'd lose it and say things she would then regret. After a long silence, she finally said, "You know, I was always taught to respect authority."

That translated to me that she probably had had a dictatorial parent who did not allow her to express herself. (In time I learned she was terrified of her father's coldly autocratic ways; she determined early in her life to hold her tongue and keep the peace.)

For some time we worked on the contrast between her father's ways and her heavenly Father's ways. One of my most gratifying experiences as a counselor was the morning when she finally was able to envision Jesus gathering her up as described in Mark 10:16: "He took the children into his arms and placed his hands on their heads and blessed them."

She cried long-pent-up tears as she experienced for the first time that she was tenderly and genuinely loved, that God's desire was to hold her in His arms and to bless her, not to criticize her or reject her.

Shortly after this sweet breakthrough, she began writing letters to God. She wrote instead of praying aloud because she still was hesitant to hear the sound of her own voice addressing Him; it was easier to write to Him than to talk to Him. I asked her to read Psalm 88 as often as she was able and to envision in the psalmist's cry her own anger that her life was "full of troubles, and death draws near," that it felt as if God had forgotten her, cut her off from His care, and thrust her "into the darkest depths," and that her eyes were "blinded by her tears."

That psalm ultimately released her feelings on several levels. To begin with, she realized she would not be struck dead if she told God how she felt. Second, she realized what a release it was for her to fully express her feelings. She didn't know how mad she was at God, but the fact that she could tell Him how she felt was liberating to her spirit as well as her mind.

She cried the pain and loss of her son until she was sure she had no more tears. But within hours, she was at it again. Each time she prayed her pain, she envisioned herself in the arms of Jesus, and He blessed her again and again with His faithful presence.

Amy never "got over" the loss of Stan in the sense that the hurt went away and the hole in her soul filled in. A deep loss remains just that: a deep loss. But she is functioning again and has an urgent desire to be an encouragement to others who have lost a son or daughter. She will never be the same; life will never be as it was. There is, however, an undergirding of strength she had never known how to access. She learned that God was with her even when she felt alone with her back to the wall. She also learned how to "cry out," understanding that doing so was being honest with God.

Crying out is telling God everything, verbalizing our deepest secrets, our strongest fears and feelings. Crying out may be cutting loose from all the restraints we thought we had to maintain in order to be spiritually pleasing to God. All that restraint does is shut us down from ourselves and shut us off from God.

We cry out for our sakes, not for God's sake. He already knows what we're feeling. But we tell Him what we're feeling for the good of our relationship with Him.

Finding Our Home in God

Humanly we feel close to the person who knows us, loves us, and does not judge us. We feel close to the one with whom we can really let our hair down. We're lucky when we have a close earthly friend with whom we can share all our thoughts. But there's no luck involved in having a divine Friend who offers this kind of solace and understanding. It's God! And He has promised to be with us and love us forever.

We don't have to pretend to believe Romans 8:28 at a time when it is totally unbelievable. God knows the moment when that is too great a stretch. If we tell Him, we don't create a distance between us. We don't have to be a phony spiritual person, afraid to admit the need to cry out with David, "I'm going down to the pit; I'm a person without strength" (my paraphrase of Psalm 88:4). We can be our honest selves with God.

I love the words of that old hymn:

> Just as I am, without one plea
> But that Thy blood was shed for me,
> And that Thou bidd'st me come to Thee,
> O Lamb of God I come! I come!

How do we come to God? Just as we are. It was more than fifteen years ago that I worked with Amy in my counseling office. What a privilege it was to walk her path with her and watch her find her way to a renewed faith. I have a graduate degree in counseling psychology, and I deeply respect the field. But I'm repeatedly reminded that psychology does not heal; God does. Psychology gives us many valuable tools, but God gives grace-laced regeneration. It is the combination of what we know about psychology and what we believe about God that provides an effective formula for healing change. Amy's life is a perfect example of that.

I understood Amy's feelings, not only because of my training but also because of my personal experience. Many years ago, when our daughter Joani was born with spina bifida, I had no background or understanding of what it meant to be honest with God, to tell Him everything, to share my secrets and my feelings as a child would do when talking to her trusted Father. I thought if I did not present to God an image of one with unwavering faith, I would lose His favor . . . Joani would not be healed . . . and if she died it would be because I hadn't "believed better."

Now, years later, I realize my agitation was increased as I attempted to carry my own burden in the name of faith. If I had "cried out," would that have made a difference in Joani's life expectancy? I don't believe that to be true at all. But I do believe God would have received my crying out and given me a peace I did not have initially. I needed a place to go and break down emotionally. What better place than in the arms of Jesus, who would hold me, receive me, and bless me.

A Homelessness of the Self

There is a homelessness of the self that we impose upon ourselves when we don't realize it is God who is our home. We know believers anticipate a mansion in heaven, but here on earth God is also our home.

It is He who provides the comforts of home, which are far more than a nice paint job and a few throw pillows. These comforts are the security of being adored—nurtured and comforted, approved of and cherished—as He walks our human path with us. The home I'm talking about is that interior space within all of us where God lives. But we become like a homeless person if we don't recognize that haven within.

When I was desperate in my prayers for Joani, I behaved like a homeless person, one who had no place to go. It's as if I stayed on a park bench and simply gritted my teeth for faith and healing for my baby. Since God is wherever I am, He shared the park bench with me, but there was a better place to be. There was a place that offered shelter, but I didn't seem to know it.

I believe many of us are afraid to cry out because we think to do so would alienate us from God. The result of that faulty thinking is that we don't go home, where honesty is rewarded and faith is increased. We stay in a homeless state, perhaps toughing it out on a park bench somewhere. What we need to do is cry out in the comfort of home.

Remember, home is that interior place in our spirits where God speaks words of encouragement to us. It's where He soothes our tattered souls and promises comfort. Isaiah 66:13 says, "As a mother comforts her child, so will I comfort you" (NIV). Home is that place where I can be real . . . where I can be honest . . . where I dare to tell everything about what I feel.

It is hard to imagine how one could leave this interior home when we carry it within us. But it is possible to close the door to that home and walk away. I've done it. Many of us don't even know we do it. But it happens the moment we, with tight-lipped determination, try to carry our own burdens, work out our own solutions, and remain stoic in the process.

Revelation 3:20 gives us an image of our interior home when we've walked away from it. This is what God says to us then:

Here I am! I stand at the door and knock. If anyone hears my voice and opens the door, I will come in and eat with him, and he with me. (NIV)

When I open the door, I've come home, and He is there. What do we then do? We celebrate with a great meal!

. . . .
Keep Talking
. . . .

1. To what degree are you authentic with God? Do you generally hide your feelings from Him? If so, why?

2. If you tell God you feel weak, will that be a sign you lack faith? If you lack faith, will He still be pleased with you?

3. Why do you need to tell God what's really going on in your emotions? What's the advantage of that honesty?

4. What is the "great meal" you share after you "cry out" to God and tell Him everything? Might the menu include bread and wine (in whatever form you choose)?

TEN

My Secret Doubts
about God

A man was being tailgated by an uptight, stressed-out woman on a busy street. When the light suddenly turned yellow, the man stopped. He could have beaten the red light by accelerating through the intersection, but he chose to do the safer thing and stop. The tailgating woman hit her horn, rolled down her window, and screamed that the man had caused her to miss getting through the intersection

As she was still yelling and screaming, she heard a tap on the passenger-side window. It was a very serious-looking police officer. He ordered her to exit the car with her hands up.

He took her to the police station, where she was searched, fingerprinted, photographed, and placed in a cell. After a few hours another policeman approached the cell and escorted her back to the booking desk, where the arresting officer was waiting with her personal belongings.

He said, "I'm so sorry about this mistake. You see, I pulled up behind your car while you were leaning on your horn, giving the man in front of you significant finger gestures, and cussing a blue streak at him. When I saw the 'Choose Life' license plate holder, the 'What Would Jesus Do?' decal, the 'Follow Me to Sunday School' bumper sticker, and the chrome-plated Christian fish emblem, I just assumed you must have stolen the car."

What do you think was going on with this woman? Was she simply one who didn't "walk the talk"? Was she a rage-aholic who cut loose only behind the steering wheel but never in church?

Here's my take on her behavior. She obviously had an anger problem, an impulse-control problem, and a major behavior inconsistency between the messages plastered all over her car and her actions. But I ask, with deliberate "*pun*niness," what's behind all that? What's the underlying secret that's hiding her real problem?

When We're Plagued with Doubts

Now I say, in all seriousness, when our behavior is so totally contrary to what we claim to believe, there's a possible problem with our belief system. Do we really, at the core of our being, believe what we say we believe? If our behavior does not reflect our beliefs, we are either well-practiced phonies or possibly persons plagued with doubts about what we claim to believe. More than likely we are both. The person who struggles with major doubts about her beliefs also struggles with her behavior because the two don't mesh; there isn't a fit. We think, *This is how I'm supposed to believe*. But secretly she admits, *Sometimes I don't think I believe any of it*. These doubts affect not only our peace but our actions.

A while ago I received a letter from a woman who was afraid her many doubts would keep her out of heaven. She had received Jesus as her Savior in her early twenties, married a Christian man, attends church regularly, and is active in her church's women's group. But she said she frequently wonders if the whole "God story" is true. Sometimes it sounds as far-fetched as a Hans Christian Andersen fairy tale.

She especially struggles with the resurrection story; it is a major stretch for her to believe it. On the other hand, she is terrified of the possible consequences of having so many doubts. She wants to be a Christian, and her fear that maybe she really is not has caused her problems with depression. She didn't feel she could share her secret doubts with any of her friends—and certainly not with anyone in her church. Instead she shared her question with me: can a person struggle with doubt and still be a Christian?

A young friend of mine confessed similar doubts

when she admitted she was bored in church, she found the Bible difficult to understand, and her mind roamed all over the place when she prayed. She feared she might not be a Christian. How can a real Christian be bored out of her mind with everything that has to do with being a Christian? Did Jesus really come into her heart and life when she asked Him to? Did she maybe miss a step or two in the process? Will she make it to heaven?

The Bible clearly states the "right steps" we take to be sure we are heaven-bound when we die. Let's refresh our minds on those steps:

1. God's plan is that you know you are loved and that He created you so that you might know Him personally:

   God so loved the world that He gave His only begotten Son, that whoever believes in Him should not perish but have everlasting life. (John 3:16 NKJV)

   This is eternal life, that they may know You, the only true God, and Jesus Christ whom You have sent. (John 17:3 NKJV)

2. The way we can know God personally is to receive Jesus Christ as Savior.

As many as received Him, to them He gave the right to become children of God, to those who believe in His name. (John 1:12 NKJV)

Behold, I stand at the door and knock. If anyone hears My voice and opens the door, I will come in to him. (Rev. 3:20 NKJV)

3. The Bible promises eternal life (heaven) to all who receive Christ.

This is the testimony: that God has given us eternal life, and this life is in His Son. He who has the Son has life; he who does not have the Son of God does not have life. These things I have written to you who believe in the name of the Son of God, that you may know that you have eternal life, and that you may continue to believe in the name of the Son of God. (1 John 5:11–13 NKJV)

These verses tell us the only way to heaven is to know Jesus, God's Son, as our Savior. If we have received Him, we're heaven-bound. If we have not, then there's always the opportunity to do that right now. A very simple prayer of acceptance can be, "Lord Jesus, I believe in You. I want to receive You into my heart and life right now. I confess my sin; I ask forgiveness for that sin, and now I open the door of my heart and invite You to come in."

Why is the confession of sin so crucial to our knowing Jesus as Savior? It is sin that separates us from Him; in fact, "the wages of sin is death" (Rom. 6:23). Sin lurks around every nook and cranny of our interior being; it especially likes to curl up and send out its infectious venom from the secret places of our hearts. And in order to be free of it, we must confess it and then experience forgiveness of it. First John 1:9 tells us, "If we confess our sins, He is faithful and just to forgive us . . . all unrighteousness" (NKJV).

So then, we do not lose heavenly citizenship when we doubt. We lose heavenly citizenship when we reject God's offer of salvation through Christ. Those steps that Scripture outlines are profoundly simple. They offer us heaven.

"Help My Unbelief!"

But now let's talk about some faulty thinking concerning the role of doubt in a believer's life. A common assumption is that doubt is sin. That is not true. Doubt is sin only if it translates into an action that rejects God. Otherwise, doubt is to question the truth of something. Doubt is not *rejecting* truth; it is *questioning* truth. To doubt is to leave room for ultimate belief.

Is it possible for the Christian to doubt and still

maintain heavenly citizenship? Of course. To be human is to at times doubt even the most basic elements of our faith. In fact, doubt can be an instrument for the building of faith.

Do you remember the exchange Jesus had with the father who sought healing for his son? In Mark 9:23–24, Jesus said to the father, "If you can believe, all things are possible to him who believes" (NKJV).

The boy's father responded to Jesus' call for belief with these words: "Lord, I believe; help my unbelief!" (NKJV).

That could be the life verse for all doubters. In other words, as the father did in answering Jesus, we can acknowledge that yes, we believe, but even so, there still are doubts. We can say, "Lord, help me with my doubts. There is room within me to experience greater belief, but my doubts sometimes threaten to swallow me up."

At one point during my health struggle with the consequences of silicone poisoning, I came to a place where my doubts threatened to swallow me up. That doubting experience was used as an instrument for the building of my faith. At the time, I did not feel the presence of God. I not only doubted His presence, I doubted His existence. This "dark night of the soul," as it was described by Saint John of the Cross, lasted only a few hours but was excruciating to me. My doubts in the past had been only minimal by comparison.

I was experiencing many physical impairments due to the silicone poisoning, which may have contributed to my spiritual vulnerability. Whatever the root cause, here's what happened.

I was sitting in a chair reading one of the psalms when I was overwhelmed with these thoughts: *This Christianity thing is total baloney. None of it is true. Why in the world am I sitting here reading from a book full of outlandish stories about a God who isn't real? Pick up a novel, Marilyn, and try to forget you're weak as a kitten, your muscles burn, and your brain keeps wandering off to la-la land, leaving you muddled.*

With these thoughts, my interior world turned black. There was no light.

I sat there in that despairing state for about an hour. Then I began to mutter to myself, "Now, wait a minute, Marilyn. There has to be a God. Only a God could make something out of nothing. How else do you explain the physical universe? It could not have simply 'big-banged' itself into existence. That makes no sense.

"And then there's Jesus. History, both secular and Christian, supports the truth of His existence; you can't deny that, Marilyn. No well-informed person denies He lived and walked the earth. All one can do is deny He was God. But it does not make sense to deny He was God. Even non-Christian historians did not know how to account for His miracles. They did not deny them; they simply had no clue how to explain them.

"Then, of course, the clincher for me is the resurrection. It is the examination of the resurrection story that has always inspired my faith in Jesus."

The Most Important Doubt-Buster

As I sat in my chair, still feeling the enveloping darkness shadow my soul, I began to go over those story facts piece by piece. I reminded myself that one of the best-supported facts surrounding the resurrection of Jesus is the empty tomb. There is solid, historical fact that the tomb of Jesus was empty on the original Easter morning.

The enemies of Jesus could have easily squashed Christianity by producing Christ's body. But they could not produce the body, so the Jewish religious leaders came up with a plan. The leaders bribed the guards to say that they had fallen asleep at the tomb and that the apostles of Jesus had come during the night and stolen the body (Matt. 28:11–15).

The holes in this story were as huge as Texas. How could the apostles steal the body? They were devastated, heartbroken, and confused. They had thought Jesus was going to become their Jewish king, establish His kingdom on the earth, and liberate them all from the tyranny of the Roman Empire. But instead, He had been murdered.

If He was God, why did He allow that? The only answer they could come up with was that He must not be God. They had made a mistake. They were all sitting on a pile of disillusionment.

Even if they did have the courage and motivation to steal the body, they would've had to get past the guards as well as move the large stone that sealed the tomb. But what would be their motivation for stealing the body? They had nothing to gain and everything to lose. Creating a hoax about Jesus' resurrection could only bring on ultimate persecution and possible death for their lie.

And if the apostles had stolen the body and created this huge lie about Jesus, why would they have been willing to die for what they knew was not even true? What would be the point?

Instead, the terrified and defeated apostles turned into courageous preachers. They became bold enough to stand against hostile Jews and Romans even in the face of torture and death.

What happened to cause them to believe as they did? They had seen the risen Jesus. In fact, numerous people (more than five hundred) had encounters with Jesus after His resurrection. These witnesses claimed to have seen, heard, and touched Jesus. The world has never been the same.

This specific event in history, the resurrection of

Jesus, started a movement that within four hundred years came to dominate the entire Roman Empire and, over the course of two thousand years, all of Western civilization.

Turning Toward the Light of the Son

As I sat there in my chair, I, too, began to sense the risen Christ. As I recounted these resurrection facts to myself, the darkness started to lift. Light slowly filtered into my soul. I knew that light was the light of the risen Christ. I was so grateful for the reemergence of my faith and the squashing of my doubt. I muttered to myself over and over again, "It's true. It's true. It's really, really true!"

My crisis of faith was a quiet and short-lived interior battle. But without it, I would not have known the drama of seeing the darkness flee from the force of that enveloping light. It wrapped itself around my troubled soul, and I began to feel restored.

Interestingly enough, it was not long after this experience that God began to heal my body of the poisons that had kept me nearly immobile for several months. Today I am still aware of the presence of silicone scattered about here and there in various organs, but I'm more aware of God's intentional resurrection power in my body. He's real. He's really, *really* real.

Secret Doubts as Smoke Screens

Earlier I shared how I was introduced to Jesus at the age of five. The onslaught of doubt hit my spirit in my early sixties. Is it possible to have doubts and still be a Christian? Absolutely. I am here to testify to that reality. But there's a better way to live than to be mired in persistent doubt.

Let's go back to the women whose letters expressed doubts that were so strong they feared they might miss heaven.

One of the writers was bored with church, Bible study, and prayer. What's the problem there?

We all struggle with our humanity, which at times does not rise to the "faith occasion." Being distracted during church or chasing after our wandering minds during prayer is troubling but also human. If, however, distraction, lack of concentration, and indifference to the Spirit of God result in consistent doubt and boredom, there is a problem deeper than our vacillating humanity. Let's do some speculating about causes.

To begin with, it is common for people to throw up a few smoke screens to distract themselves from or cover up the real problem that is causing them to doubt. One of those root problems may be not wanting to lose personal control. An interior dialogue might sound like this: *I don't want God to get a hold of my life . . . . I don't want to give up what I'm doing . . . He might want me to do something I don't want to do . . . I want to be in control . . . I can keep Him at arm's length by simply saying I have a lot of doubts . . . it doesn't make sense, and I can't help it—I'm bored.*

Another smoke screen may be based on anger at God and what He has allowed to happen. This was the case in my other doubting correspondent. It may be easier for her to blame away her lack of spiritual contentment to problems with doubt instead of owning up to her problems of resentment with God. Facing God in her vulnerability would mean she would have to respond to the force of His love. Perhaps she no longer trusts that love and does not want to risk trusting it again. It's easier to just remain a doubter. Less is required . . . it's safer.

Now let's take a step back and speculate on what in their backgrounds may have resulted in these women's troubling doubts. Unfortunately, parents often shape our ideas about who God is, how He behaves, and what He expects of us. If these women have a parent who gave little room for failure, it may be frightening to attempt a relationship with God. They may fear disappointing Him by their inability to "do it right." It's easier to be a doubter than to risk His not being pleased with them.

The first woman may also have a temperament prone to melancholy. It's difficult to have a happy faith experience when nothing in life makes a lot of sense or even holds much promise for meaning. For a melancholy temperament, faith is not the only challenge; sometimes life itself is.

Both women may insist that if all their doubts and questions are not answered satisfactorily, there is no choice but to remain a doubter. They can't enter into a faith-walk unless there are no questions. They must have proof in order to believe. They must have proof before they can clear out the doubts.

All these smoke screens boil down to one basic emotion: fear.

- Fear that God will take away personal control

- Fear that God might melt the anger barrier

- Fear that God may find a less-than-perfect-performance person

- Fear about everything, believing life is hard

- Fear that God doesn't have the answers for doubt

A Matter of the Will

The absence of fear does not mean doubt disappears. But facing those fears and realizing they are smoke screens to faith is a positive step in the direction of moving from doubt to faith. Actually, for those of us who don't relinquish control easily, here's a comforting thought: faith can be a matter of the will. I can will to believe, or I can will to not believe. The choice is mine. That means I can choose to live with faith rather than fear.

John 7:12–17 describes an interesting incident in which Jesus talked about the strength of the will:

> There was much complaining among the people concerning Him. Some said, "He is good"; others said, "No, on the contrary, He deceives the people." However, no one spoke openly of Him for fear of the Jews. . . .
>
> The Jews marveled, saying, "How does this Man know letters, having never studied?"
>
> Jesus answered them and said, "My doctrine is not Mine, but His who sent Me. If anyone wills to do His will, he shall know concerning the doctrine." (NKJV)

Jesus encouraged the unbelievers who were surrounding Him in the temple that they could "[will] to do His will." If they did, they would know who authored the doctrine about which Jesus spoke. He was encouraging them to a place of personal willingness.

John 12:37 also records a revealing incident regarding the will as it related to the many miracles Jesus performed before the people. It says, "Although He had done so many signs before them, they did not believe in Him" (NKJV).

Despite the miraculous visual witness of God's power, there were many who simply willed against what they saw and what they had no explanation for. They chose to not believe. They were not even doubters; they were unbelievers. The doubter leaves room to be convinced of truth. The unbeliever turns from truth.

I remember a time when my heart was touched by a doubter. There was room in her heart for truth; she did not turn away in disbelief. The occasion for this experience was with a newspaper reporter assigned by her editor to cover our Women of Faith conference in their city. She was to interview me during one of our Saturday morning breaks. She came to the interview with a look of total disinterest. She had no desire to talk to me and even less desire to cover something with the corny title Women of Faith.

After a few preliminary questions, she looked me straight in the eye and said, "Can you prove absolutely the existence of God?"

I looked into her gray eyes and said, "No . . . I cannot absolutely prove the existence of God. But there's enough evidence in favor of believing in His existence to tilt me into the camp of faith."

She put her pen down for a moment and stared at me. Then she said, "You really believe it, don't you?"

"With all my heart," I responded.

She softened; we talked.

She had come in to do a quick interview, write the story, and be gone. Instead, she stayed for the rest of the day. Her spirit was moved. She wrote an enthusiastic story that made the front page of her large and influential paper. Faith was making moves on her.

You may be one upon whom faith is making moves. You may have kept your doubts secret or shared them with everyone who would listen. And now your doubts have caused you to cry out. Your back is against the wall, but remember: while you are there, with your back against the wall, God shares the wall with you. Psalm 94:19 is a tender reminder of God's love for the doubter: "When doubts filled my mind, your comfort gave me renewed hope and cheer."

If you struggle with doubt, I'd like to make a few suggestions that may contribute to your "renewed hope and cheer":

֍ Be assured that you do not lose your heavenly citizenship when you doubt.

֍ Make a conscious decision about your doubt: do you will to believe? If so, you're going to need the Author of your belief to help you. Say to Him, "I will to believe. Help me with my will. Please strengthen it, focus it, enable it to do what I can't do in my human weakness."

🎗 Study the object of your faith. Read the Gospel of John over and over and over again. (I suggest John's Gospel because it has the greatest number of Jesus quotes.)

🎗 Get involved in a Bible study where you are safe and will not receive gasps and groans when you honestly share your doubts.

🎗 Keep a prayer journal. Write your prayers to God. Then read your prayers out loud to Him. This will help you corral your mind and your concentration when you talk to Him.

🎗 Go to church. Jesus went to church, and I can't imagine how He kept from being bored. After all, He knew more than anyone there! But He went to worship. There is a sweet spirit of worship that settles over the soul when we all come together for that purpose. If the sermon is a challenge to your attention, take notes. It will help you remain focused. If the sermon cannot be outlined and has no sequential flow, perhaps your pastor should take English Comp 101. (Forget you read that last sentence.)

Finally, let me say to those of you who want all your questions answered, that day will never come this side of eternity. The sixteenth-century mystic Madam Jeanne Guyon wrote:

> If knowing answers to life's questions is absolutely necessary to you, then forget about the journey. You will never make it, for this is a journey of unknowables—of unanswered questions, enigmas, incomprehensibles, and most of all, things unfair.

Our challenge is to love Him for what we do see and trust Him for what we cannot see. Rising to that challenge may prevent us from tailgating or losing our tempers when the law-abiding driver ahead of us stops at a yellow light. Our doubts may occasionally persist, but they do not have to dictate our behavior. It's more fun when faith does that.

Keep Talking

1. Do you think a person who struggles with doubt is really a Christian?

2. Do you think doubt is a sin? Can you say that you don't doubt God is real, that Jesus is your Savior, and heaven is a real place?

3. Talk about a specific time of doubt in your life. How was your faith restored?

4. Imagine yourself comfortably sitting at a table with Jesus, sharing a cup of tea and expressing your doubts to Him. How do you think He would answer you?

ELEVEN

Revealing Your Secrets, Transforming Your Thinking

We've talked a lot about marriage in this book. Perhaps it's turned out that way because when we consider how dark, destructive secrets can impact our relationships with others, the marital union easily serves up a wide variety of examples. The truth is that marriage was designed by God as a relationship of intimacy, but too often it deteriorates into a painful trap of secrecy.

Rocky marital relationships are far too common in our present-day culture, and as a result, marriage gets a lot of bad press. One cynic said, "Marriage is a lot like the army; everyone complains, but you'd be surprised at the large number that reenlist." That quote reflects our contention that the greatest longing of the human heart is for relatedness. If it doesn't work the first time, reenlist with someone else. Consider the following letter.

Dear Marilyn,

I am forty-one years old and have been married two times. Each marriage ended in divorce. I am embarrassed by those failures. I'm also surprised I keep trying. Neither of my husbands cared much about God but didn't seem to mind that I do.

I'm a Christian and want God's will for my life. What am I doing wrong? I prayed about both marriages.

I really want to raise my three boys in a good home. Both husbands were unfaithful to me, and both were physically abusive. I'm sure all this is my fault. I'm engaged to be married again, but now I'm scared. We've been living together for a month, and he already shows a mean streak. He hasn't hit me, but he yells a lot. My oldest son says he hates my fiancé. I keep praying, but I don't get any answers.

—Cold Feet

Now, let's pour ourselves another cup of tea and talk about this situation. The first thing I would say to Cold Feet is, sweet baby, where are you looking for answers? What kind of answers do you want? The Bible answers a question you don't seem to be asking. You should not be living with your fiancé. You should not be having sex with him. Why? Read 1 Thessalonians 4:3–5: "God wants you to be holy, so you should keep clear of all sexual sin.

Then each of you will control your body and live in holiness and honor—not in lustful passion as the pagans do, in their ignorance of God and his ways."

Just in case you need additional scriptural support on this subject, read 1 Corinthians 6:18–20:

> Run away from sexual sin! No other sin so clearly affects the body as this one does. For sexual immorality is a sin against your own body. Or don't you know that your body is the temple of the Holy Spirit, who lives in you and was given to you by God? You do not belong to yourself, for God bought you with a high price. So you must honor God with your body.

Now, honey, those Scripture verses are so clear, you don't even need to pray about them. You just need to obey them. They are requirements about how we all are to be living. You say you are a Christian and want God's will for your life. There you have it, baby. I suggest you move out.

I appreciate how open you've been in laying out your history. It lets us identify an obvious pattern in your marriages. You marry nonbelieving, abusive men. Is that kind of man your only option? Are there no choices here for you? Do those choices work for you? The answers are no, no, and no.

Remember, your "body is the temple of the Holy

Spirit, who lives in you and was given to you by God."
You can't go marrying people who bash the temple of the
Holy Spirit. That's a huge no-no. Just as you are to honor
the temple by being sexually pure, you are to honor the
temple by protecting it from these cavemen types who like
to hit, beat, and diminish a woman. You can't allow that.
You "honor God with your body."

God wants to transform you by changing the way you
think. I'm afraid you think you deserve to be abused.
That's why the men you have chosen in your life are all
abusers. Somehow, you think that's right for you. That's
wrong for you.

Was your father abusive? Did he yell, kick, hit, and
scream? Often, the children of a home where this painful
situation existed learned—or were forced—to keep secret
the terrible things that were happening. Later, those secrets
reappear and take control of the adult child's life. If this
has been your experience, my guess is you are continuing
to live out what is familiar to you. Abuse is familiar, and
even though you may hate it, you continue to choose it.
It feels like home. Once again I say to you, "Move out."
Figuratively speaking, you are still living at home.

Let me tell you what God would have you think about
yourself. You are His child. He's crazy about children.
Jesus, the visible God to us on earth, surrounded Himself
with children. When the disciples tried to shush them out

of the way so Jesus could do the "important" work, Jesus reprimanded the disciples. Mark 10:13–16 shows us the tenderness of Jesus:

> One day some parents brought their children to Jesus so he could touch them and bless them, but the disciples told them not to bother him. But when Jesus saw what was happening, he was very displeased with his disciples. He said to them, "Let the children come to me. Don't stop them! For the Kingdom of God belongs to such as these. I assure you, anyone who doesn't have their kind of faith will never get into the Kingdom of God." Then he took the children into his arms and placed his hands on their heads and blessed them.

Since God wants to transform you by changing the way you think, let's consider what He wants you to think. He wants you to think that not only are you His dearly loved child, but He loves you with tender compassion. Psalm 103:13–14 reads: "The LORD is like a father to his children, tender and compassionate to those who fear [reverence] him. For he understands how weak we are; he knows we are only dust."

Sweet baby, I suggest you close your eyes for a moment. See the image of Jesus blessing the children, tenderly placing His hands on their heads. Then see yourself as one of the children in that group of little ones surrounding Jesus. Feel His touch on your head. Rest in this image again and again, every day. God wants to transform your thinking. You are loved. You are worthy. You are precious to Him. See the image and say the words until you begin to grasp their transforming truth.

Remind yourself that God is not judging you. "He knows how weak we are; he remembers we are only dust" (Ps. 103:14). Tell yourself that even in your past weakness, you have been loved, are loved, and always will be loved. He will enable you to change your poor-choice patterns. His desire is that you will be able to provide a good home for your family. He adores you; He adores your boys. Read His Word, listen to His voice, and rest in His arms of comfort. "The eternal God is your refuge, and his everlasting arms are under you" (Deut. 33:27).

Now do what you know you need to do. Partner with God as He teaches you new ways of thinking. Life can be richer and sweeter than you have known it to be—and better than you could ever imagine it to be.

Share the Secret, Shed the Guilt

It has been said that growing old is like being increasingly penalized for a crime you haven't committed. Whether it's growing old or feeling responsible for every wrong thing that happens in life, many of us are toting a load of guilt we haven't earned.

I had a friend from at least 382 years ago who was constantly apologizing for things she had nothing to do with. Here's an illustration. Our junior high graduation was scheduled to be held outside. It rained. My friend was beside herself with regret and apologies. For one thing, to schedule anything outside in the state of Washington is inviting a wild run for tarps and umbrellas. Someone obviously made an administrative blunder, and that's the person who should have been "awash" with regret and apologies, not my neurotic soon-to-graduate little friend. Instead, she refused to come into the gym until every bedraggled thirteen-year-old had sloshed his or her way through the door and sat in hastily arranged chairs near an empty stage.

One could assume my hand-wringing classmate was simply compassionate and caring. She put the needs of others ahead of her own needs. Isn't that an admirable quality? I for one liked that quality because I knew she'd never take the last Hershey's Kiss. But the reality is, her seemingly generous spirit had its origin in not feeling "good enough." In fact, she was so "not good enough" that somehow rainstorms were her fault. She was so "not good enough" that in her mind, any bad thing could somehow be traced to her. I see the same thinking pattern in Cold Feet when she wrote to say, "I'm sure all this is my fault." *Whatever is wrong in life, I've caused it and I must work like crazy to fix it.*

Cold Feet has made some extremely unwise choices, and she needs to take responsibility for those choices and work toward changing some patterns. But her choices reflect her lack of self-esteem and the belief that she does not deserve to be treated with respect and kindness. My junior high school friend's behavior reflects her unspoken but lived-out belief that *everything* is her fault. Both beliefs spring from the same source; in the dark, secret corner of her heart, neither woman understands her inheritance of love and value.

How does a person get that way? As you might expect, it goes back to childhood messages. Those messages get taped in the little tape recorder that plays relentlessly in our brains. For example, "I'm not good enough" is first communicated through the senses of the infant. There are no words for that recording, but there are sensory messages that the infant tucks away for the day when there are words.

The first year of life is when the little one comes to feel whether she is good enough. Good enough is com-municated by touch and sound. When Mama is impatient and rough and ignores the baby's crying, the infant gets the message, "I'm not good enough to be held, cuddled, or sung to . . . It's got to be me . . . Something is really wrong with me!"

The first year of life is when trust of the environment is established. It's when the infant learns it is possible to receive comfort and love and not rejection or abandonment. To routinely leave a baby endlessly crying is to create a sense of fear, abandonment, and worthlessness. Ultimately, that sense of worthlessness grows as the child grows. If the messages continue to be apathetic or negative, the sense of self is, "I'm not good enough, and that's got to be my fault."

Those messages need to be changed. That thinking needs to change. That's why I suggest that Cold Feet envision herself among the children Jesus tenderly touched and blessed. She needs to retape the messages in her head. She needs to hear messages that speak to her of her value, her worth, and her many lovable qualities.

And, since we're telling each other everything over our cups of tea, here's another pattern that seems to dog our footsteps. We marry the person who originally hurt us (Mom, Dad, or both) in an effort to heal old childhood wounds. In marriage, we unwittingly re-create the conditions of our upbringing in order to correct what our early pain was.

In other words, if Dad hurt me, "I'll marry someone like him, but the one I marry won't be like him after all.

He'll be kinder, and gentler. We will be able to talk, and I can express my feelings without being afraid like I was when I was a kid. The one I marry won't abuse me but will instead love me and value me the way I always longed for."

The irony here is that the abused one all too often seeks out further abuse because it's all she has known. Even in trying to correct the childhood pattern, she may not trust any other pattern, so she returns to what is predictable and familiar. Understanding this reaction is the first step to changing the pattern and transforming her thinking.

Keep Talking

1. Why do we act in ways that are contrary to what we know to be best for ourselves?

2. What destructive behaviors or habits do you see in yourself that could have their secret root in a hurtful experience from your childhood?

3. What does God's Word say about how He feels about you? Do you have to earn God's love and acceptance?

4. How can you avoid the rocky relationships that plague many modern-day marriages and instead create the love-filled openness and intimacy God wants your marriage to have?

TWELVE

Bringing Secrets from
Death's Darkness to the Light

John 11 provides a graphic and memorable account of a dead man. His name was Lazarus. He and his sisters were close friends with Jesus. Their home frequently provided a place for food and rest for Jesus as He traveled in the area. When Lazarus got sick, the sisters frantically called for Jesus to come, but by the time He arrived, Lazarus had been dead for four days.

At Jesus' request, Martha, one of the sisters, led Jesus to the grave. It was a cave with a large boulder sealing its entrance. When Jesus commanded that the stone be rolled away, Martha protested and said, "Lord, by now the smell will be terrible because he has been dead for four days" (v. 39). But in obedience to Jesus, she had the stone rolled away. And guess what happened next.

"Jesus shouted, 'Lazarus, come out!' And Lazarus came out, bound in graveclothes, his face wrapped in a headcloth. Jesus told them, 'Unwrap him and let him go!'" (vv. 43–44).

What in the world is that story about? And why is it included in a book about bringing dark secrets into the open and living a life of openness and honesty?

Here's why: We've said repeatedly in these pages that God wants us to have a good and abundant life, an existence that is better than anything our most vivid imaginations could concoct. Yet too many of us are instead living in misery—in direct opposition to what God wants for us. One reason for this misery is that, like Lazarus, we are entombed in a grave.

Lazarus was entombed because he had physically died. Scripture says we are dead because of our sin. Ephesians 2:1 states, "Once you were dead, doomed forever because of your many sins." And 1 Peter 4:6 says, "The gospel was preached also to those who are dead" (NKJV).

Breaking out of our tomb means repenting of our sins. The key to an abundant life in Jesus is to open up our grave of secret (and sometimes not-so-secret) sins, confess them, talk about them, repent of them, and let the redeeming light of His love burn away the infection they have caused.

Scripture describes those who have not received Christ as dead people . . . dead in their sin . . . dead because they have no spiritual life. At one time we were all a Lazarus, bound up in graveclothes, dead and stinking in our sins. But then Jesus called us to life. We have been called from the grave of sin to a new state of spiritual life.

As we step out into that new life, Jesus invites us to, "Tell Me everything." Then, no matter what kind of sordid "secrets" we pour out to Him (secrets that were *not* secret to Him in the first place), when we ask Him to forgive us, He promises to do so.

Did Lazarus have the will, the determination, the ability to roll that stone away, throw off the binding graveclothes, and walk out into the sunlight? Of course not. How did he do it? He was called by Jesus. He was called from death to life. You and I also have been called from death to life. Our will or determination or personal abilities have nothing to do with that calling. As *The Message* puts it, "It's God's gift from start to finish!" (Eph. 2:8).

It is also God's gift that enables us to live our Christian life without tripping over our own graveclothes. Jesus said to unwrap Lazarus and let him go. He says the same thing to us.

But then we sometimes get bound up in graveclothes again. The dark secrets start up again. It happens when we refuse to admit our powerlessness, clam up, and refuse to open our hearts to His cleansing love. It happens when we think our walk with God will be successful based on our abilities instead of His.

We're All Failures at Rule Keeping

God's people learned about their powerlessness when they received the Ten Commandments. At first they thought it felt good to know just exactly what it would take to make God happy. All they had to do was follow the rules, keep God's laws. Then they discovered they could keep some of the laws but not all of them. They could stop themselves from murdering but not from envying. They could stop themselves from adultery but not from lusting—and on and on.

God knew all along they couldn't keep the laws. He wasn't doing a "nah-nah-ne-nah-nah" to His people when it dawned on them they were failing at rule keeping. God knew they'd fail at it. The point of the law was to show His people they needed a Savior. They could never make themselves good enough for God. He demands perfection. The Old Testament law was intended to demonstrate to the people their inability to be perfect.

Doesn't it seem odd then that the desire for rules persists in our thinking today? We understand we are no longer dead. We understand God demands perfection, which we couldn't achieve, so Jesus did it for us. We understand that the Holy Spirit lives within us and is our power source. But in spite of that knowledge, we reach for the graveclothes and bind ourselves up with a list of rules. Maybe your list of rules would look like this:

1. Read the Bible every day (minimum thirty minutes).

2. Pray every day (minimum thirty minutes).

3. Join a church.

4. Be baptized.

5. Serve on church committees.

6. Stop drinking.

7. Stop smoking.

8. Stop swearing.

9. Give a portion of income to the church and other Christian organizations.

10. Cut back on chocolate.

11. Memorize five verses (minimum) of Scripture each week.

12. Never criticize or gossip.

You may now have stopped the hammock, dropped the Milk Duds box, and started thinking, *That's a long list, but I think I could do it (except for the chocolate). All it would take is a disciplined regimen and determination.*

The Lure of Legalistic Discipline

If you're thinking that way, you've already slipped into the trap of self-effort and self-motivation. That is not trusting Him enough to let Him do it. You're attempting a program where the emphasis is trusting yourself, and that's a form of legalistic discipline. You're planning to follow the rules and counting on your personal discipline to carry it off.

Legalistic discipline is about obligation. It's about "doing it right." When our life is driven by obligation, we soon lose our desire to talk to God, to revel in what He did for us, and to assume a "trusting Him enough to let Him do it" attitude. Legalistic discipline causes us to be too busy with the timer during Bible study, prayer, and Scripture memorization to enjoy our new life as a Christian.

Also what is sobering about legalistic discipline is that it not only refits us for graveclothes, but it refills those dark corners of our hearts with destructive secrets and sends us back into the tomb. We're not dead, but it feels like it. We're not really buried, but we feel trapped.

But that's not what Jesus wants for us. He called us out of there, and He also said to get unwrapped.

The subtle lure of legalistic discipline is that it looks good. There's nothing wrong with the rules we listed. In fact, they are rules we may want to consider. No, the problem with rules is not the rules themselves but how we determine to keep them: through obligation to God or through love of God. If it's obligation, sooner or later we're going to tire of feeling obligated. Sooner or later our well-intentioned discipline will fail us. Why? Because in ourselves, we are weak.

That brings us to the subject of my thumbs. (Of course it does, Marilyn! You're so easy to follow.)

Over the last few months, I've developed increasing discomfort and a new weakness in my thumbs. When I need to take the cap off a water bottle, for example, I wander helplessly about in search of an able-bodied thumb person. What's that about? I'm told it's arthritis.

Understanding my new weakness, would I benefit from the discipline of at least thirty minutes of thumb exercises a day? Would I find a measure of relief by increasing my determination to twist off the tops of water bottles without a grimace? How many times a day should I repeat my efforts at the non-grimace cap-twist? Just what is my obligation to my thumbs? Mercy!

A Life Based on Love

The opposite approach to living out our new Christian life is based on love for God and not obligation to Him. Jesus said in John 14:15, "If you love me, obey my commandments." He did not say, "If you don't keep my commandments, your children will have crooked teeth for the next four generations." He didn't say, "You better do what you're told, don't ask questions, and keep those commandments perfectly."

There is no threat in Jesus' statement. There is an assumption that love produces a desire to obey. He knows you're going to mess up. You don't have to—in fact, you can't—hide your mistakes from Him and sink into secrecy, thinking your outward actions are the basis for His attitude toward you.

You see, our love for God, our appreciation that He called us out of deadness, inspires a genuine eagerness to read the Bible, talk to Him in prayer, and memorize verses that are personal, portable power packs for our "dailiness." Because I love Him, I want to attend church, share my earnings with Him, and address those behaviors that have produced ungodly habits. That desire springs from love, not obligation.

That love of God is the key to trusting Him enough to let Him "do it." Do what? Everything! Absolutely everything. The joy of responding to God's love for us comes in the partnership He offers us in overcoming our difficulties. We are not alone in them. He partners with us by providing the wisdom and strength—and even abstinence from those life issues that threaten to derail us. In our love for Him, in our trust of Him, we receive from Him all we are not. This is what it means to "let Him do it." He invites us to climb off the treadmill of self-effort and rule keeping.

Partnering with God to Overcome Our Secrets

I'm in periodic correspondence with a woman who secretly struggles with alcoholism. She is a pastor's wife in a relatively small community. One of her greatest fears is being "found out." She knows all the scriptures, and she knows God has not disowned her. But the grip of alcohol continues its hold upon her.

How would this woman let God "do it" for her? Would she just choose to head for a hammock and substitute Milk Duds for a bottle?

Letting God "do it" is not a passive action. We partner with Him. He has the power; we do not. We recognize His power, and in our powerlessness we pray, "Jesus, help me!"

That He *will* help us is a given.

What is the pastor's wife's responsibility in letting God "do it"? She needs to choose to trust Him. She also needs to admit her powerlessness. Oddly enough, she thinks it's only a matter of time before she's able to "conquer" her vice. She's working on increasing her discipline. She's also tripping over her graveclothes.

He didn't call her to rule keeping, even about something as destructive as alcoholism. He called her from death to life. He called her to a partnership of trust. In that partnership, she can experience the power to overcome. Philippians 4:13 states, "I can do everything with the help of Christ who gives me the strength I need."

So can you. So can I. That's the role we play. It's not the major role. God plays the major role while we rest in who He is and what He has done and in the knowledge that we were, are, and will always be the focus of His love. And that powerful love is what brings us from death to life.

Keep Talking

1. Do you see yourself as a Lazarus? How?

2. Do you trip over your graveclothes? If so, do you know how and why?

3. Read the whole story of Lazarus in John 11. Why did Jesus wait to come to Mary and Martha? How do you feel about His reasons?

4. Do you have any rules you think you need to follow? What are they? Why are they important to you? Are they necessary?

5. What is a legalist? Is there a problem with legalism?

Where would you feel most comfortable: with a set of rules that made it clear what you should or should not do—or trusting your love of God to direct your behavior?

It's No Secret—Christ Lives in You!

There's a knock on Saint Peter's door. He looks out and a man is standing there. Saint Peter is about to begin his interview when the man disappears. A short time later there's another knock. Saint Peter gets the door, sees the man, opens his mouth to speak—and the man disappears again.

"Hey!" Saint Peter calls after him. "Are you playing games with me?"

"No," the man's distant voice replies anxiously, "I'm in a hospital, and they keep trying to resuscitate me!"

This poor guy didn't know if he was coming or going. My hope and prayer is that you will have *no* uncertainty about the direction your life is taking. I hope you'll feel absolute assurance of God's love for you, His total forgiveness of all your sin, and your worthiness to be a member of His family. It's a done deal! There's no waffling on God's part. You belong to Him, and He won't let you go.

You will have times, as we all do, when you will feel overwhelmed by your circumstances and even scared for your future. When that happens, don't come and go in your faith in the Father. Instead, listen and be encouraged by these words from Philippians 4:

> Don't fret or worry. Instead of worrying, pray. Let petitions and praises shape your worries into prayers, letting God know your concerns. Before you know it, a sense of God's wholeness, everything coming together for good, will come and settle you down. It's wonderful what happens when Christ displaces worry at the center of your life. (vv. 6–7 MSG)

Christ not only "displaces worry at the center of your life," He *lives* in the center of your life! And He doesn't make a secret of it.

ABOUT THE AUTHOR

$\mathcal{M}$ arilyn Meberg speaks each year to 350,000 women at the Women of Faith conferences and is the author of several books. Never one to avoid the hard questions of life, Marilyn Meberg shares the wisdom she's gained from two master's degrees and a private counseling practice.

new from WOMEN *of* FAITH

BEAUTIFUL THINGS HAPPEN WHEN A WOMAN TRUSTS GOD

By Sheila Walsh, wherever books are sold

In a message rooted in hope and substantial Bible teaching, Sheila Walsh helps women to see the beautiful things that can happen in their own lives and in the lives of those they love when they fully trust their heavenly Father during good and bad times.

NOTHING IS IMPOSSIBLE

Wherever books are sold

In this Women of Faith devotional, women will encounter page after page of encouragement, humor, insight, and teaching to rediscover the God who will not let them go.

KALEIDOSCOPE

By Patsy Clairmont

Acclaimed author and Women of Faith speaker Patsy Clairmont causes women's hearts to leap and their hopes to lift in this quirky, straight-to-the point look at the Proverbs.

TELL ME EVERYTHING

By Marilyn Meberg, available 3/30/2010

With the wisdom of a counselor and the whit of a comedian, Marilyn Meberg untangles the issues in women's lives that hold them back from a vibrant relationship with Christ.

FRIENDSHIP FOR GROWN-UPS

By Lisa Whelchel, available 5/4/2010

Former *Facts of Life* star Lisa Whelchel shares her experiences of growing up without true friends, how she learned to find and develop them as an adult through God's grace, and how readers should actively pursue meaningful friendships as adults.

DOING LIFE DIFFERENTLY

By Luci Swindoll, available 5/4/2010

An inspiring account of Luci Swindoll's courageous life that teaches readers how to live savoring each moment, how to let go of regrets, and how to embrace dreams.

THOMAS NELSON
Since 1798